GW00986552

We Are Still Here

Rebecca Liebermann Nissel

MEMOIRS OF A CHILD OF SURVIVORS

We Are Still Here

By

Rebecca Liebermann Nissel

gefen
publishing house
JERUSALEM • NEW YORK

Layout: Marzel A.S. — Jerusalem
Cover Design: S. Kim Glassman

ISBN: 965-229-374-1

Edition   1   3   5   7   9   8   6   4   2

Gefen Publishing House, Ltd.   Gefen Books
6 Hatzvi St.   600 Broadway
Jerusalem 94386, Israel   Lynbrook, NY 11563, USA
972-2-538-0247   1-516-593-1234
orders@gefenpublishing.com   orders@gefenpublishing.com

www.israelbooks.com

Printed in Israel   *Send for our free catalogue*

"A clan and a family resemble a heap of stones: one stone taken out of it and the whole totters."

— *Bereishit Rabba* (Midrash)

Contents

Acknowledgments

This book is the end result of a long process of listening, internalizing and composing. I had an immense desire to hear family stories from an early age. The next step was writing, many times on the telephone with my father and mother; first on scrap paper, then learning how to write by taking numerous classes and filling spiral notebooks. Finally came editing what would make it into my book.

It was Shoshi Bitton, a young talented lady who helped me with the initial editing and I thank her for all her help.

Many times when I had to read my stories in class I could not continue to read because my emotions just over took me. That's when I realized how important these memories were. I knew that whenever I cried it was good; it needed to be told.

It has been a lifelong effort, and without the help of certain people who over time explained to me that my stories are in a fact a book, I could never have accomplished it.

Ilan Greenfield at the head of Gefen Publishing House with a group of fine assistants helped me to publish this book. I would like to thank Ilan from the bottom of my heart.

I am grateful to the Gefen team: Smadar Belilty, project coordinator; Leah Stern, marketing and public relations; Kim Glassman, a talented artist, for helping me to find the perfect book cover; Kezia Raffel Pride, my editor, who was extremely patient with me and reminded me at one point that I have to let go of the stories; they would stand on their own.

To Rachelle Benevista, a great writing instructor who throughout the last few years taught me how to write a story.

I have to thank Joe Bobker, who published a lot of my stories in the *Los Angeles Jewish Times*.

Also Naomi Mauer, who published my stories in the *Jewish Press*.

I thank the *Los Angeles Times*, who printed a few of my opinion pieces.

My sister-in-law Miriam Liebermann, an accomplished writer who gave me the courage to do what she had done for years before me: to write.

I have to thank my sister Mona; she is an integral part of my book.

My brother-in-law Ruben is an excellent editor who helped me with correcting final pieces that were sent out for publication. He introduced me to the magazine *The New Yorker*; reading it inspired me to continue writing.

My brother Tomi is a positive spiritual force in my life.

I would like to thank my oldest son Tzvika, a wonderful writer himself, who also read my stories and helped me a lot with the computer.

I have to thank my middle son Chaimi, who with my lovely daughter-in-law Dahlia gave me my first grandchild Eli; he continually inspires me to write about how beautiful life is.

I thank profoundly my son Erez, the youngest of my children, who from an early age loved to read. He too patiently read my first attempts at stories.

The book's whole raison d'être is definitely my parents. May G-d protect them with good health.

The last person I have to thank is my dear husband Raphy, my partner for the last thirty-three years.

Ha Kadosh Baruch Hu — I am grateful to G-d that He let my parents survive the horrors of the Second World War and with this sustained the miracle of our heritage.

1. *I Am the Bridge*

It was Passover. Maybe 1958. I was a little girl of about five or six. I remember sitting on my father's lap while Papa moved his knees up and down in tune with my favorite song, "*Dayenu*," a basic passage of the *Hagada*. As children, my brother, sister and I were encouraged to ask as many questions as possible, to make it an exciting evening. Why do we eat the hard-boiled egg? Why do we eat the potato or the parsley? Why do we dip everything in salt water? Why do we lean to the left when we eat? Why do we have to drink four cups of wine? Why do we eat matza instead of bread? Why, why?

Little did I know that with this specific evening my life would change forever.

From all the explaining and singing my father got hot and turned up his long-sleeve shirt. The blue number A16303 was partially covered by body hair, but still visible to my young eyes, and attracted my attention.

"Why do you have a blue number on your forearm?"

I interrupted my father's singing. He looked

at me and answered after a pause, "A long time ago bad people came to my hometown in Romania and they gave me this number. Instead of my name they called me A16303."

I don't think that I understood at that moment the impact of his answer. But it ignited a tiny flame, like a pilot light in a stove, that would burn for the rest of my life.

My book is an attempt to convey to my reader what I saw, and still see, in the eyes of my father after he has a nightmare and what I felt while growing up when he told me stories of the terrors he lived through. Even now, I continue to ask questions; constantly, waiting patiently for the right moment to approach my father. I deeply feel that one of my purposes in life is to tell my family's story; not just my father's story of survival, but the story of how he celebrates life to its fullest. Memories of how he found our beloved mother Ildiko and how she survived the war and later taught us children to see the purple lilacs in the park, how to draw pastels and how one can enjoy reading a good book on a snowy Sunday afternoon. It is the times of total joy that I wish to convey.

I want to share how graceful and beautiful my life was thanks to my parents who saw themselves not as victims of the Holocaust but as human beings who wanted to heal the next generation with love, beauty and light. Yet, in doing this I also must express the pain and

My parents' wedding picture, 1950.

anger I saw in my father's face when we encountered Nazis on the streets of Vienna, years after the Holocaust. I vividly remember how once, an older woman with a Tyrolean hat on her carefully coiffed white hair thought that as a Jew, my father should clear the narrow sidewalk for her Dachshund. I pulled and begged my father to stop yelling at the woman. I knew she would never stop hating the Jews, but he screamed and yelled at her till he was blue in the face. He let out his pent-up frustration on one person who represented the hatred instilled in a people for thousands of years.

And then there were also the nightmares. Even though I was surrounded by song most of my life, how could I ever forget my father's screams at night when he had his reccuring dreams of horror. He constantly relived the selection by Mengele in Birkenau, and the mock hanging he endured for stealing tooth powder for his older sister who lost her teeth due to neglect. I knew my mother would wake him up and talk to him in a soothing voice reminding him that it was all over.

"Nussi, Nussi, wake up, it's okay, it's okay," she said, and quieted him down until the next nightmare unfolded.

I also had nightmares as a little girl, but I knew that I could not slip under my father's cover for comfort. His sheets were drenched with sweat from his nightmares; sometimes my mother had to change the sheets daily. Every morning I saw the pink dahlias piled up on the blue carpet, all shrunken and sad from absorbing Papa's bad dreams. She stopped using the hard-to-iron linen and pillows that she received from her family as a wedding gift. The ones that had her initials stitched on them with white thread: "I" for Ildiko and "K" for her maiden name Kelemen.

Much later, when my father came to visit my family in Los Angeles, it happened again.

"Papa, wake up, you are having a nightmare. I am here."

He stared at me blankly for a second, like he could not recognize me, and then smiled.

"I am so glad you woke me up. Tomi was just about to walk to the left."

Drops of sweat formed on his forehead and I handed him a tissue from the plastic bag on his nightstand. And then he told me his dream.

My sister and brothers asked ourselves many times, over and over, "How can we be the same after what our parents had to go through?" How could they, five years after the war, smile at the photographer as if to say, "Look at us, we are the happiest people on earth!" How did my mother dress up in her glittery silver lace gown, put on makeup and go hand in hand with my father to see *The Merry Widow* at the opera on New Year's Eve? I loved watching my mother in preparation for an evening out at the opera. In

My mother attending a Jewish ball in Vienna,
wearing her famous tiara, about 1960.

these moments I did not see a trace of sadness in her lovely face, only beauty. My parents instilled in me a love for music for which I am very grateful. When I listen to Verdi's *La Traviata*, I slip into the beautiful world of opera and forget everything around me. I nod at the old man sitting next to me in greeting, even though I wonder if he might be one of the men who controlled the valve of the gas chamber that killed my grandmother in Auschwitz.

In the last thirteen years I began to record these important stories. I admire the generation of survivors and the way they built up their lives so quickly and efficiently after the war, without looking back, just going forward one step at a time. Young men and women sailed to their Jewish homeland to build a country, others traveled for days on ships to America and some stayed in Europe. My parents got stuck in Vienna, Austria. Many times during my upbringing I asked myself why we never moved away from this country that brought so much misery to my people? I asked my parents this question over and over, but I never received an answer that was to my satisfaction.

It was a fellow classmate, Susie, who finally made me understand why we stayed in Vienna.

It was in 1972, the day we waited for Professor Kautz, our high school teacher, to enter the room and reveal all the important facts about the final exams everyone had to pass before entering university. They were highly regulated tests under the strict supervision of the Ministry of Education.

I gripped the plastic cover of my bright red calendar as the teacher announced the dates. I opened it and my heart sank. The French test was scheduled on Rosh Hashanah, the Jewish New Year. Immediately after class I approached Professor Kautz.

"Is there any way the authorities could change the date for the French test? I have to attend synagogue services on that day. It's Rosh Hashanah, our New Year."

"*Ja, Ja,*" she replied, "I know you are one of those observant Jews... Let me see what I can do about it. I will let you know in a few days."

Eight years of high school... I had worked hard to reach these final months and could not imagine sitting alone on a bench facing the inspector, a stranger from the Ministry.

The days passed and finally Professor Kautz entered the classroom and called us to order. "We are going to vote today in class," Professor Kautz said. "We could postpone the final exam to another date, so that Rebecca can participate together with the class. As some of you already know, she celebrates a Jewish holiday on this date. Everybody in favor of postponing the exam please raise your hand."

My classmate, Susie, broke the silence. "Let

Rebecca attend Jewish school, then we won't face any problems."

"But, there is no Jewish school in Vienna," I said, trying to defend myself. "Don't you understand? We are a minority in this city. My parents outlived millions of people in the war and they don't have the strength to build schools. They work and work, only to survive." I mumbled these words because I never spoke up for myself like Susie did.

I sank back into my Jewishness and only faintly heard the announcement from my teacher that she would ask the authorities to postpone the test date.

This incident made me understand the purpose of my father's presence in Austria much more. It was a clear message to everyone.

My dear fellow Austrians, my father's voice still rings in prayer, and I am here to tell his story, to record it, and make sure that it will serve as a foundation for our children's lives, as it did mine. Just as we sit at the Seder table every Passover to retell the story of redemption, so too our story will be told and never ever forgotten.

2. *The Auschwitz Coat*

"After Auschwitz-Birkenau, I was separated from the few members of my family who were still alive and was shipped to Stutthof in a cattle wagon," my father told me. Stutthof, near Danzig, was a transit camp in Poland for inmates on their way to and from other concentration camps. The Nazis seemed to be forever shipping people from one place to another.

"I was lucky," Papa continued. "When I arrived at Stutthof I still owned an Auschwitz prison jacket. I recognized Dukee Grun from my hometown, Cluj (Romania). Dukee and his brother Zoldi were natural entertainers. Zoldi did the *gramen* (an entertaining and sometimes comical improvised song about the bride and groom) at my sister Peru's wedding in Decz. Dukee was a magician. He was also an experienced Stutthof inmate. He welcomed me and gave me important instructions on how to survive the next few weeks. As we talked he fingered my precious coat and kept staring at it for quite a while. Finally he said, 'If you give me your jacket I will teach you the art of magic in return. I know which of the inmates have food and I entertain them with magic tricks on lonely nights. That's how I earn an extra ration of bread. I will tell them you are my assistant and this way you will always have something to eat. Is it a deal?' I readily agreed. From my experience at Auschwitz I knew that deals like this were vital for survival.

"Most of the people who were in the camp with us were Jewish, but some of them were Polish criminals who, unlike the Jews, had the privilege to receive parcels of food from their families. These were the ones that we entertained. They were willing to share their rations of food for a fleeting moment of happiness.

"I remembered watching Dukee do his magic tricks at the open marketplace in Cluj. He would approach the farmer women selling eggs and carefully remove one from their basket. He would crack it in two and magically a five-Lei coin would appear from inside the egg. Their mouths dropped open in amazement. They would ask Dukee to repeat the trick over and over again. After a while they were sure that all their eggs must be magical and so instead of selling them, they cracked each one open in hopes of finding another valuable five-Lei coin. They would have been better off selling their eggs, but to me it proved that Dukee was an excellent magician and putting myself in his

My grandmother Toby was gassed in Auschwitz-Birkenau. This image of her as a young lady is the only picture of my grandmother.

hands would be worth suffering in the cold without my jacket.

"In that dreadful camp Dukee's gift helped me survive. In the few hours we had inside the barracks we would change the people's depressed grimaces into smiles. I was the one who chose the object Dukee made disappear and reappear. I would pick a metal drinking cup, a small wooden spoon or useless piece of paper; anything I thought would do the trick. We did not have much to choose from in those barren barracks. Dukee's magical fingers would wrap around the item I picked and enthrall the inmates. Sometimes he draped a rag over it or at times the article would just disappear into the sleeve of my old jacket. 'Ah! Oh!' they would cry out and clap their hands with admiration. That's when I realized that my jacket was saving us from more than the cold.

"But most of the time the SS guards made us stand outside; the torture could last for up to eighteen hours at a time. From the moment I arrived at Stutthof and throughout the four weeks I spent in that dreadful camp there was a constant downpour. I don't know how or why. Maybe it was because we were near the Baltic Sea, but it seemed more to me like the heavens were crying for us because we were unable to cry for ourselves anymore. People died of exhaustion and hunger and pneumonia from the wet clothes that would never dry. They dropped like flies. Life drained out of their weak bodies. Skinny legs like sticks stood deep in mud, hunched over like they were carrying the burden of their people on their backs. Cold and drenched from those heavenly tears we stood and stood. Ghostly figures leaned against the background of the little barracks which we used to rest our tired bones."

Rest was one of the precious basic commodities denied to the prisoners. When someone leaned against a wall during roll call, a guard would shoot him on the spot. When the inmates finally sank onto their bug-infested beds, which were no more than planks shared with another prisoner, they were often treated to another torture during their few precious hours of sleep. The gypsies had fun exchanging the shoes which were lined up in front of the bunks. When the exhausted inmates were whipped out of bed in the middle of the night — called to stand for roll call starting at 3:30 in the morning — instead of slipping into the muddy wooden slippers they had received at arrival, some of them would have a left shoe three sizes smaller than their feet and a right shoe several sizes bigger. Nobody had time or strength to look for the right size of shoes. Barefoot, they continued to stand for hours till most of them gave up and sank dead into the mud.

"We were twelve hundred poor souls when I arrived at Stutthof and four weeks later when I

Sister Malki with husband Chaim and their four children all perished in Auschwitz. Family of Chaim.

left we were one hundred. If not for Dukee, who gave me an extra piece of bread, I would not have been strong enough to survive those rainy weeks."

Listening to my father on the phone in sunny California, I feel the bitter cold of Stutthof penetrate my bones. I wonder if it is still raining in Stutthof? I need to see with my own eyes. I want to see the muddy everlasting imprints of my father's fellow inmates. I want those who suffered to know they did not wash away for nothing. I am listening.

3. Bread for Passover

My father's bones shattered.
The Nazi hit him so hard
For a piece of bread he took from the Polish inmate.
Bread to celebrate Pesach.
He felt no pain then
He said his bones were used up
No more pain.
Bones once abused, now brittle.

He heard the whip.
A hollow echo stemming from close by.
He told me his bones made music.
Was the sound reaching heaven?
G-d heard the bones give in.
And liberated Papa two days later.

The sounds of the French trumpets
Sang the Marseillaise.
Today he broke his hip
Those poor bones have to heal.
They've suffered so much.
Please, G-d, help those bones!
Papa has to get up and
Go to shul!

(Written by the author in 2005 when visiting her father who broke his hip.)

A piece of bread stuck out from Jan's rucksack, hidden in the low ceiling of the bunk in the concentration camp "hospital" at Vaihingen-Enz, Germany.

"Yidl, can you hear me?"

"Yes, Nussi, what do you want, I am too weak to talk."

"I just realized that tonight is the first day of Pesach. Look up, that's bread up there; let's get a piece in honor of Pesach. Jan is in the hole again, where he spends most of his time these days, and it's a shame to let that food rot away."

Jan was a Polish inmate, a criminal, maybe a thief or a murderer; nevertheless the Nazis allowed him to receive packages from his family back in Warschau.

There were only a handful of Polish prisoners. They hated the Jews and collaborated with the Nazis to secure better treatment. Jan had a strong stomach virus, which caused him to spend more time in the hole than in his bunk. He could not hold any food down, but spitefully, he would not give anything to his dying Jewish inmates; he'd rather let the food waste in the rucksack. Every day the strong aroma of homemade sausages, Emmenthaler cheese and Gugelhupf — a sort of cake — tortured their noses.

"You are right, Nussi, let's have some bread. Quickly take it before Jan comes back from the hole."

Papa grabbed the bread, which was in easy reach for him, and broke off a piece. Together they lay on the bare wooden plank that was their bed, too weak to sit, ready to have a Seder.

"Let's start with the ceremony, 'read' the *Hagada*, and sing '*Ma Nishtana halailah hazeh, mikol haleilot?* (Why is this night different from all other nights?)'"

Papa broke the piece of bread in two and handed a part of it to his friend. A quick glimpse at the door — they did not hear Jan's footsteps yet. They chewed the bread slowly, indulging in the taste, swallowing only after the bread melted on their tongues. When it was all finished, they insisted the bread had taken on the taste of matza.

"Nussi," asked Yidl. "Your family had a bakery in our hometown, Cluj. Tell me something, how does one bake bread?"

The bread was gone and Yidl wanted to daydream about food so he closed his eyes.

"Well, Yidl, first you need a few ingredients: flour, yeast, water, a little sugar, maybe some eggs and oil. You put them in a bowl and mix them up well, but then comes the most important part. The dough has to rise, and this can only happen when it's covered with a towel positioned in a warm place. My mother would put it next to the large ovens. After a few hours she would place the dough into a loaf pan and then put it into the oven. The heat from the oven transforms the sticky goop into warm delicious bread. Can you smell it, Yidl?"

At that moment Jan returned from the hole.

My father's first picture after liberation and many months at the rehabilitation centers. With his friend Yidl who helped him survive, 1946.

He always checked on his rations first and this time he noticed something was missing. The rucksack was not as bulgy as before.

"Herr Oberstumführer, come quickly," he screamed, "those dirty Jews stole my bread!"

The *Oberstumführer* heard the commotion and entered the bunk with the whip in his hand. "You stinking, rotten Jews, when will you learn to obey orders? Fifty lashes each!"

As he whipped my father's bones it made a strange noise, like when hitting a hollow tree — no insides, nothing. Papa heard the *cling-clang* and yet he did not realize that it came from his own body. Despite the fact that he was a slave he still wanted to celebrate the holiday of freedom, Passover.

"Yidl, can you hear me, we had a nice Seder, the matza was delicious, it was all worth it."

4. *The Angels Had Warm Feet*

The heat near the smokestack was unbearable. They burned six hundred thousand Hungarian Jews in Auschwitz within a six-month period.

"The Nazis started deporting us right after Passover. That's why I always talk about it around this time." I quickly grabbed a paper and pen while my father continued talking to me on the phone.

Day and night smoke filled the sky. The orange flames shot up very high.

"It was always dark, but not like the darkness of night; it was as if a huge cloud was hovering over us, souls that weren't ready to die. It was there my entire stay in Birkenau. I did not know if it was time to say *Shacharit* or *Maariv*, morning or evening prayers, but *tefillot* — prayers — were always needed in a place like that. The awful stench penetrated my eyes, ears, nose and skin. At first I tried covering my mouth with a rag — I couldn't breathe — but then I slowly got used to it, the smell that is. It was part of Auschwitz and part of me. Like the lice that moved in with me, too."

The ovens worked twenty-four hours, non-stop, no break. The souls of thousands reached the heavens in a short period of time.

"The angels must have had warm feet. They must have had warm feet from all the heat and fire that came out of the main smokestack. They guarded the gates to heaven and received

My father's sister Peru as a young girl.

the children with outstretched arms, thousands upon thousands; and they were ready to embrace them. My nieces and nephews, eight all together, none of them older than eleven years, they were cradled by the angels; they were too little to be left alone. They believed in G-d, they had *emunah*, faith. On their way to the crematorium they sang, '*Ani maamin, ani maamin* (I believe, I believe).' They were received with open arms in heaven."

I gave up writing things down. I couldn't write when the tears filled my eyes and made the pages blurry. But I still remembered what he said.

"I did not understand how the neighbors in the nearby city of Auschwitz did not smell the stench. The entire area was under a cloud of dark gray with small stains of orange, blue and yellow. Ashes fell on us like snow, touching us lightly. These ashes must have landed on the next-door farmhouses too, on their roofs, chickens and hens. But nobody came to see where the fire was coming from."

As my father continued unburdening his heart, a new part of the story, one I had never heard before, emerged. "It's hard to imagine that I had almost been a part of creating that cloud. A few days after we arrived in the camp the SS officers asked for volunteers to work in the 'bakery.' My father thought it would be something good for us to do; we owned a

Grandfather Shrager Zvi Liebermann with son-in-
law Yankl Avraham, Uncle Czumi and my father
(half in the picture). This is one of only 2 pictures of
my grandfather.

bakery back in Cluj. We knew we wanted to stay together so we promised that if only one of us would get picked the other would run back to Bunk 25, our assigned bunk."

Listening closely, I was filled with awe that my father still remembered his bunk number.

"The next day when we lined up, I was the only one picked. I waited until the guard was not looking in my direction. Then I ran and ran without looking back. I collapsed in my father's arms. Till today I believe that those angels protected me. If not for my father's desire to remain together, I would have been tricked into burning Jewish souls instead of baking bread. I would have been part of the *Sonderkommando*."

I could not imagine the horror my father would have felt entering the crematorium and being hit by the tremendous stench of burned flesh instead of the familiar sweet smell of bread.

"There were those who fell into the trap. Mr. Pollack, an employee of our bakery, was part of the *Sonderkommando*. He was the last one who saw my aunt alive."

"'Today I burned my boss,' he told my father. 'I wrapped her carefully and said Kaddish.'

"Our family died *al kiddush Hashem*, for the sanctification of G-d's name…" said my father as his voice trailed off.

5. *The Miracle*

The command post in Berlin gave their last order. Anybody who could walk, anybody with an ounce of strength left in their broken bodies, had to get up and walk to the nearby woods. It was the Nazis' last attempt to herd the leftover souls to a nearby hill and shoot them. Papa crept on his hands and knees, faintly hearing the commands shouted in German, *"Heraus, heraus, alle mussen heraus!* (Out, out, everybody out!)"* My father had no idea what the rush was; he saw a tunnel, and light at the end of it, then abruptly the shouting and yelling interrupted his hope of reaching the light. He moved slowly, the same pace as the rest of the emaciated bodies.

"Geht schon ihr Schweine, schneller, schneller! (Walk, pigs, faster, faster!)"* The yelling and screaming of the Germans sounded like machine-gun rattling. They were in a hurry to get rid of the last witnesses.

Dr. Mittler, a friend of my grandfather's, had kept Papa alive to this point. He would whisper encouraging words: "I hear them coming, I hear the thunder of the tanks and the bombing of nearby villages. We did it. Hold on. Stay alive." Incapable of moving, drained of all life, he remained wrapped in his thin blanket; but Papa did not hear his friend as he continued to crawl out of his bunk on his hands and knees, following the other lifeless bodies in a single line. He felt like a tiny spider clinging to its web.

"Nussikam, come back, come back. Stay with me," Dr. Mittler pleaded. "Don't leave me."

Instinct, that's all, instinct and a longing to be back on his bunk to rest his tired bones, that's what made him stop crawling along with the ghostly figures that were on the way to the *Todesmarsch* (death march). "I think I was even too weak to crawl. That's why I turned around and crawled back to my friend Dr. Mittler. Let me tell you, I was nineteen years old, but I felt like I was ninety."

One of the storm troopers noticed him: "*Schau, der schmutzige Jud kriecht weg!* (Look, the dirty Jew is crawling away!)"

"*Lass ihm, der ist schon tot!* (Leave him, he is already dead!)" said another soldier.

My father made it back to the bunk and joined Dr. Mittler, whose weakness had glued him to the boards. It was his comforting words of freedom that encouraged Papa to hold on. Though they were heard faintly, they kept him alive in those last few hours before the liberation.

There are only 2 photos of my grandfather, Shrager
Zvi Liebermann. In this one he is sitting. Next to
him: son-in-law Yankl Avraham who is next to my
father's oldest brother, Schleume-Chaim
Liebermann. The other person we don't know.

About half an hour later they heard shots
and that's when Papa knew what a miracle it
was that he had turned around. The shooting
didn't stop for a long time.

"There were a few hundred of us who had
almost survived the war but were hastily buried
in a mass grave along the river Enz."

And then it was over. The French came, and
it was over. My father had survived the war.

"After the French liberated the Vaihingen-

Enz concentration camp, they transported me to Karlsruhe, a small town nearby where they had converted the Nazi headquarters into an infirmary. They made the Germans nurse us back to life. They would not let me die."

After that Papa was transported to Heidelberg, where a castle had also been transformed into a makeshift rehabilitation center. "Again I don't know how many months it was until they released me. But I have this little ID card that I carry around with me until today. It says that I was released on August 20, 1945."

I held the thin worn paper in my hands; it felt as if it would disintegrate at any moment.

My father stayed in a hospital near Stuttgart for many weeks, till his stomach was able once again to digest solid food. Too many of the survivors, who did not receive the kind of care my father got, died from trying to eat normally too soon.

The recovery was slow. It took months till they opened the hospital doors and said, "Go home and look for your family!" This was all he had thought of from the moment he realized that he was still alive. He received a train pass good for any train in Germany, in order to find members of his family. At that point he still hoped that his father had survived and maybe a few of his siblings.

Papa traveled all around the country, searching papers in DP camps and talking to people in order to receive any kind of information.

Finally he arrived back in his hometown in Romania. There he found out that his father had died just two days before liberation in a concentration camp near Munich. His brother Schleume-Chaim with his wife and two children died in the gas chamber. His older brother Czumi, who jumped from the moving train on the way to Auschwitz and survived, was waiting for him together with three sisters, Eidi, Feigi and Mindu. His sister Peru with her husband and two children, and his oldest sister Malki with her four children also died in the gas chambers. My father had watched Malki's husband Chaim fade away before his eyes in Auschwitz.

"Chaim could not get over the fact that his wife and children were gone. Within a few months, sorrow shrunk him into nothingness," my father once told me.

"Rebecca, if not for the doctors and nurses at the sanatorium center, I could have had the same fate," my father told me.

My father always credited the French doctors with having saved him. It was at his sixtieth birthday party, many years later, that Papa revealed the one mistake the doctors had made.

My father insisted on having a huge party for this birthday. We planned a big gathering in a hall next to the only kosher restaurant in

Vienna and invited all his friends. As the party drew to a close Papa got up and spoke:

"When I was in the sanatorium after liberation the doctors were determined to keep me alive. They wrapped me in cotton, like precious porcelain, and fed me from a baby bottle for weeks. They commanded the frightened German prisoners to delouse me. Gradually they brought me back to life. But, before I left to search for my family, one of the good doctors said to me, 'Mr. Liebermann, you'll be a lucky man if you manage to live till sixty.'

"I am happy to announce to you, my dear friends, that today is December ninth and it is three days after my sixtieth birthday. The doctors were wrong! I am still here; you are my witnesses."

6. *Colored Stones*

At the age of six my mother had figured out that the ruby was her favorite gem. I heard the story of my mother's childhood in Budapest many times but I did not mind hearing it over and over again. Each time she told me about the times before the war, she would remember some little detail that she had never told me before. To me, it was like digging for treasure. With each shovel of earth another precious memory was revealed. I was on the phone with my mother when another glimpse of the past emerged.

"When the Nazis marched into Budapest and deported my mother to Bergen-Belsen, a family friend, Mr. Sloboda, gave me strict instructions to make my way to the town of Buda in another section of Budapest where my grandfather's nursemaid, Anna, was supposed to take me in. The morning I woke up to the loud shouting noises in the street I knew they were rounding up the Jews and I had to hide. I knew what to do. My friends and I had all memorized what our parents taught us to do when the Nazis came; we had mentally rehearsed every move. Each one of us had a different strategy for survival.

"After waiting in the attic between two doors for hours I slowly descended out into the open street. All I had was a tiny piece of paper with the nursemaid's address on it, but I had no idea how to get there. I bumped into a bunch of young men who belonged to the Hitlerjugend, the Hitler Youth. They wore black knee-high boots, brown uniforms, and had pistols in their holsters. They did not intimidate me, though. I had a new identification. I was Eva Kovacs and not Ildiko Kelemen. I wore a gold chain cross around my neck and I was young and beautiful. I boldly asked them if they would accompany me all the way to this lady's home because I had no idea how to get to the other side of the Danube where the town Buda was. These young Nazis walked me to the tram station, ascended with me, and kept me company the entire way to this lady's home. On the tram I watched people crossing their chests and in order not to look suspicious I did it too."

As Mutti filled in details I remembered the beginning, the story of her ruby-filled childhood. She would never play in the park like the other children in her neighborhood, who pushed each other down the slides and flew high on the swings together. Her favorite thing to do after school was to sort out precious

My mother and her older brother Riczi.

My mother with my grandmother and Riczi,
her older brother.

stones in my grandfather's jewelry store on Kiray Utca. She would delicately finger the sky blue sapphires and grass green emeralds, golden brown tiger-eye, the deep blue lapis lazuli, the striped malachite, the sparkling aquamarine and deep purple amethysts. But the blood-red rubies were her favorite. With the exception of sewing beautiful doll clothes, there was nothing else she loved doing more. It all was so familiar to her; the bell that would ring announcing customers into the store, and the light blue soft cushioned Louis XIV chairs placed on the inlaid parquet floor. But the most beloved and familiar of them all was the wooden box with tiny compartments that made my mother's job child's play.

"Artists who were hired to create the most delicate pieces of jewelry for valued customers would come to our store. Sometimes, instead of discarding their leftover stones, they would hand me the ones with a small crack or chip in them. They were not perfect for their intricate work, but to me they were priceless. I would place each treasured stone into its own compartment of the wooden chest. To protect the unique stones, each little cubbyhole was upholstered in luxurious plush beige velvet. While my grandparents and mother were busy selling wares to our customers, I would be playing in the back of the store. Many times when my mother called me to dinner I had a hard time parting from my fantasy world.

"'Ildiko, time to go home for dinner, it's almost seven,' she would call.

"'Anyu, I am almost ready, I just have to put away the malachite.' That was always how it went."

I realized what an education I received from my own mother simply from hearing all these stories in person or on the phone. It was incredible to think about the luxurious surroundings she grew up in and how ironic it was that during the war, she had to exchange those special childhood stones for a piece of bread or jam.

"I saved myself during the war by selling one stone after another. I was fourteen when my mother and grandmother hastily sewed the beautiful stones into the hem of my overcoat, dress and undershirt, before they were taken away.

"'Never ever hesitate to buy food with these stones; survival is the most important thing,' they told me as their hands worked quickly inserting the rubies, diamonds and other gems into my clothes. When the nursemaid and I had run out of food I would go out into the streets and try to buy food on the black market. I would remove an emerald, diamond or ruby out of my skirt and buy what I needed. I clearly remember the homemade jam I got once. You don't know how many times I dreamt about and craved jam during those hard times. A large diamond bought that luxury.

"Before the Jews were all forced to move into the Jewish ghetto I would sneak out to visit my grandmother's Swedish safe house and bring her food. But after a while things got too hard. The Russians bombed day and night and I was not allowed into the basement with Anna. Someone would have realized I was a stranger. A friend and I stayed in the basement of the last house in the Jewish ghetto. One night when we were really hungry, we broke through a wall into the neighbor's apartment building. We found a storeroom full of food. Floor to ceiling shelves bent from the weight of the jars and cans. We went back and forth bringing with us pickles, fruits, sardines and sauerkraut. This is how we survived until the Allied troops rescued us."

Mutti was lucky she survived. No, she was not in a concentration camp like Papa, she was not beaten, she was not a slave worker, and she did not have to watch her mother walk into the gas chamber. She had a different way of surviving. She lived by her precious stones; she lived by giving away her precious childhood memories one by one.

7. *The Hidden Holy Room*

Cold. Cold. The coldness took my breath away. The year was 1996. My husband and I decided to take our children to Eastern Europe to trace our roots. We sat in the old Kazinczy Synagogue in Budapest on Yom Kippur night. There was no heating, although it was almost zero-degree weather. The cold penetrated my skin and ran deep into my bones. The chill reached into my heart and into my soul. This was the synagogue in which my mother had spent many happy years while growing up.

The echo of the *chazzan's* (cantor's) voice vibrated throughout the three-story building. Most of the colorfully stained windows were broken and the wind rattled the brown wrapping paper that filled the empty window frames. I looked up from my *machzor* (High Holiday prayer book), trying to imagine my mother walking through the giant oak doors and ascending to the women's section on the second floor where I sat. The warmth of her mother's and grandmother's hands protected her. Did she sit in the middle section or on the side? Maybe she sat on the very same chair where I sat? Did she also notice the magnificent architecture of this synagogue or was she too young to be aware of its beauty? I looked up at the ceiling. It was supported only by wood beams that were held up by iron chains. Where was the sky blue cupola with gold stars my mother had described to me?

There were about ten women near me in the ladies' section, mostly elderly people who were not looking in their prayer books. It was as if they didn't know how to follow the service. Where were the ladies dressed in long gowns, decorated in their finest jewels? Where were the men in top hats and black coats carrying canes in their hands made of pure silver? Where was the diamond pin on my grandfather's tie? I looked around at the ladies dressed like they had just returned from running errands. Where was the elegance my mother had described?

Yom Kippur morning, before I took my seat I began wandering around the forbidden grounds on the third floor. A sign on the railing warned me to turn around; the balcony was not safe anymore. On my way up I almost stepped on an old *machzor*. I picked it up and carefully wiped away a few layers of dust. I read the inscription on the inside of the cover.

"November 1943 — To my darling daughter

on the occasion of her Bat Mitzvah. Many kisses, Your mother."

Great-grandfather and great-grandmother Heiden on vacation in Karlsbad.

Was this writing my grandmother's, inscribed for my mother? I wondered if this *machzor* was connected to me — who had cried tears in it? With it in my hands I walked onto the balcony. It was in shambles. Collapsed broken seats with faded red velvet upholstery were leaning against the walls and lying on the floor. The voice of the *chazzan* reached up to where I stood. I looked down. A bird's-eye view revealed about fifty Jews in the men's section, the remnants of an Orthodox community of thousands.

I continued opening the doors on the third floor. I was searching for the past. The last door in the attic revealed a sight I will never forget. On the right side of the tiny room were four antique *aronot hakodesh* (closets to hold the Torah scrolls). There were no precious Torah scrolls in them; they were empty. Printed sheets of Jewish texts were stacked up high on an antique wooden table in the corner. Completion of their publication was probably forced to an abrupt stop with the Nazi occupation. Heavy old trunks and chairs held piles and piles of Jewish books. My black suit was covered in dust. I picked up many books, searching for inscriptions, trying to find a name that belonged to my mother's family. I couldn't find any. I felt like they had been erased.

Hooks on the wall held rags that had once been curtains for the Torah arks. A green velvet *parochet* (curtain) was thrown over a wooden pole. One large hook pierced a burgundy velvet curtain, reminding me of a cow at slaughter. Rays of sunlight peeked through the broken windows illuminating the gold-embroidered *Magen David* (Star of David) on the burgundy-colored *parochet*. I felt the remains of a past holiness. Here was the majesty my mother had described. Slowly I descended to the second floor, trying to hold onto those feelings while I began to pray.

I reached deep into the history of the Hungarian Jews by going to that synagogue and all I found left was the skeleton of a thriving community. As a young girl, my mother had a beautiful, rich life in Budapest filled with lovely memories that she often shared with me. She was always careful to leave out the unpleasant part of how when she turned fourteen her life of fairy tales was turned into one filled with tragedies. She didn't want to have nightmares; she wanted to leave all that in the past. Only much later did those tales of horror reach my ears.

My entire family said *Tashlich* (a special prayer of repentance said over natural water during High Holidays) on the shores of the Danube River after Yom Kippur. I stared at the watery graveyard that had swallowed up so many of the worshippers whose prayer books I held in my hands at the Kazinczy Synagogue. I stood there before the holiday of Sukkot, a specific remembrance of our total dependence on G-d, and I prayed for those whose souls were taken as a testimony of their own beliefs. As I walked away I felt their faith strengthen mine.

8. *Mami Sleeping*

As a child, decked out in a blue plaid skirt and white cotton blouse, I did not like going to school. The thought of getting up at seven in the morning, in the middle of winter when icicles formed on the windows and it looked like it was still night outside, still makes me want to curl up under my covers a bit longer.

"It's dark outside, I want to sleep longer," I would protest to my mother, who was still half asleep herself.

Until this day, it's a mystery to me how my mother managed to get up that early. She never wore a watch and we never had clocks hanging on walls or any other place. Mami slept when she was tired; it did not matter to her if it was daytime or nighttime. During the day she went to her store to sell her wares, dresses, sweaters and T-shirts whenever she felt like it. Occasionally a salesgirl would come to guard the store. My father hired her so that my mother had a chance to sleep when she felt like doing so.

Mami accomplished a lot of work at night,

such as sewing the velvet dress I wore to my cousin's wedding or taking care of the store bills. Everything was so much better on days when Mami had gotten a good night's sleep. First of all she was in a good mood and cooked wonderful meals like Palatschinken with strawberry jam or Hungarian beef goulash or Krautfleckers or Marillenknodel. All that was produced with ease when Mami was not tired. Mami ate when she felt like eating; and if she craved a piece of broiled chicken at two in the morning that's when she would eat it.

When Mami walked into my room in the morning, she was asleep. Her eyes were closed, and she mumbled something like, "You have to get up and go to school."

As she continued her sleepwalk into the kitchen, she prepared my Butterbrot for snack in school. She must have opened her eyes to cut the slices of bread with a knife that was too sharp to use blindly. But many times I watched her lay the butter on the dark bread with eyes shut tight against the intrusion of daytime. Her dark hair covered her forehead and her quilted robe was buttoned the wrong way. She always wore a small, worn-out angora sweater over her robe to keep her warm in the cold kitchen early in the morning. She stood there on the green and white linoleum tile floor dipping a tea bag into a glass, her last act for my sake before she snuggled back under her duvet cover.

"Drink your tea before you leave, it's below zero degrees this morning," she would say as she spooned some sugar into the cup and handed me the reddish-brown hot liquid as we walked to the door.

I did not argue with my mother too often about how I hated to get up so early and go to school, because I knew she was tired and wanted to go back to bed as quickly as possible. But once in a while Mami felt sorry for me and let me sleep in for an hour or two. At least then it was not dark outside anymore and it was easier to get up. I knew my teacher would ask for a letter of excuse for the tardiness. So, before I left home I wrote on a clean piece of paper: "My daughter Rebecca Liebermann should be excused because of a headache. Sincerely," and then my mother signed her name. Mami wrote only in her native tongue, Hungarian; all German correspondence was written by her children. At times I switched the headache for severe stomach cramps, which I had just thinking about getting up that early.

I loved Mami for the fact that she did not put up a fuss when I really wanted to sleep in. If she had anything to say about the school schedule, she would vote for it to start at noon and end at four in the afternoon. That made much more sense to her. But she believed that her children should have a good education, study hard and achieve their goals for the future. And so we left at seven in the morning despite the cruelty of the hour.

Sometimes, when I was too tired to study for a test, she said, "Here, lie down a bit on this couch, rest a while, then I'll wake you up and you'll feel all better to study." Mami believed that one had more energy after a short nap and could do much better work after that. She said that it was important to listen to one's body and realize how much rest it needed.

I always wondered how Mami made it on time to school for all the parent-teacher conferences and school plays I performed in, like the *Barometermacher auf der Zauberinsel* or *Die Palatschinkenpfanne*. Sometimes she called the automated time service on the telephone. But as a child I believed that Mami had swallowed a watch like the crocodile in *Peter Pan*. She had a built-in time system that directed her to school for events and everything else she cared about. I must say Mami never missed out on anything that was important to me.

Today living in Southern California one does not have to deal with dark freezing mornings. But, at times, while raising my own children, I remembered how good it felt to sleep in once in a while, and wrote them an occasional letter of excuse for their tardiness. And when my sons felt too tired to study, I gave them the same advice my mother told me: "Take a half-hour nap on the black couch in the den; I'll wake you up and then you will have much more energy to study."

They listened to me. I also still follow my mother's rule when errands become too much, lists of "To-Do's" get longer and longer and I don't know how or when to start. I simply snuggle under my favorite checkered woolen blanket on the black leather couch, and lo and behold when I wake up from my nap my list of errands is always still there right where I left it.

9. *Carnival on Ice*

I was not allowed to move, otherwise the needles would prick my arms and legs. My mother held five needles between her lips as she fit the shiny white brocade fabric snug against my body; slowly I became a Hungarian princess for the Carnival on Ice extravaganza.

"Maybe I should just sleep with this dress, Mami, there is no way I could ever get out of this without removing hundreds of your needles," I said to her. My mother mumbled something which I was unable to understand since her mouth was full of those prickly things. She was concentrating deeply on the gown. Mami had placed a full-length portable mirror in front of me so that I had a chance to admire the elegant heavy fabric that was draped around me. I touched the rich material and dreamily pretended to be walking down the large staircase of the castle just like Empress Sissy did in the movie I had watched a few weeks before.

Every winter during ball season in Vienna the artistic side of my mother blossomed lavishly. When I was six I attended my first ball.

Since then my siblings and two first cousins anticipated the approach of ball season with me as well.

Carnival on Ice was one of the main delights our mother brought to us every wintertime. My mother's creativity was boundless and we would float along with her in a fairyland of her own creations. For a short period of two days we reveled in the joy of entering her fantasy world. In a matter of two or three days, she created the most beautiful and magical costumes with her own hands. Sometimes we would become a Spanish prince or princess, a Hungarian hussar and his mate, or a Thai prince and princess. But, no matter what she created, we paraded in our costumes with great joy and pride.

My mother was inspired by the art she saw in museums, theaters, or the ice-capades she often attended. Rembrandt was her favorite, though. The rich fabrics, textures and colors of the curtains and costumes she saw at the opera prompted her imagination also.

"You don't even listen to the opera; you only look around at the gilded balconies and admire the clothes," my father would say to her after they had attended an elegant evening of listening to *Fledermaus*. Sometimes when I went with her to the theater I would watch as she would draw little sketches of the beauties she saw before her. These were her muses for the luxu-

(From left to right) My cousin Eidi and my sister Mona dressed as Thai prince and princess, cousin Gabi dressed as a Dutch girl. My brother Tomi dressed as a Hungarian hussar (soldier) and I as a Hungarian princess, 1963.

rious and unique costumes she made for us to wear at the Carnival on Ice.

We were actors in her fantasy creations, active participants in her dream world. "I've got it," she would say with great enthusiasm when suddenly she knew who would become what for the magical event.

"This year, Rebecca, you and Tomi (my younger brother) will be a Hungarian hussar and a Hungarian princess. You, Mona (my older sister), and Eidi (my cousin) will be a Thai princess and prince." As soon as the decision was made my mother immediately began to work on her new project. That same evening she would come home with the most magnificent fabrics and accessories. I will never forget the hush lingering in our living room when Mutti revealed the treasures she had bought for the carnival while we were in school.

"Wash your hands and I will show you what treasures I found for you." Before we did anything we always had to wash our hands. There was heavy silver lamé fabric rolled on the table. Sometimes it was gold or silver lace, artificial fur, beads and pearls, or sequins in shiny bronze tones. Thousands of shiny rhinestones in deep purples, emerald greens and burgundy reds were tucked away in little bags for us to slowly open. And then to our delight Mami piled up rolls of ribbon in all colors of the rainbow onto the table. We were silent as we watched her beautiful hands reveal one surprise after another. She talked while she showed us her treasured items. Her imagination raced ahead of us in full force. She saw the final creation in front of her eyes, before she even began the first stitch.

She had never really been formally trained as a seamstress, but she worked wonders with her Singer sewing machine. The magnificence of her designs really came from her most prized possession: an incredibly talented pair of hands. Caught in a flurry of creativity, she could switch from the right to the left at any time. For two days and two nights prior to the event she did not sleep at all. During the night she would pin and drape the fabric on wooden mannequins she had bought in a second-hand shop. I distinctly remember the slow rhythm the machine would make as she lightly tapped and released the foot pedal. The undulating rhythm lulled me to sleep.

Upon waking, we would walk into the living room anticipating what a glimpse of Mami's masterpieces would reveal. "Ooh!" and "Ahh!" were the only sounds we could make as we examined our costumes. It was impossible for me to imagine that she had completed so much in one night by herself; it was as if *Heinzelmänchen*, elflike creatures from one of our best-loved fairy tales, had assisted her as we slept.

"Try it on, Rebecca," she would say to me as she helped me into the costume. Before putting on the skirt I pulled on a crinoline slip that she had made the previous day. The underskirt was made of a stiff fabric with wires pulled through to give fullness and shape to my gown. The skirt was a cream-colored brocade that had a silvery shine to it. The top was a heavy silk material in the same color as the skirt. The sleeves were puffy and were gathered at the wrists with elastic. On top of the blouse I wore a red velvet vest; gold ribbons crisscrossed in the back and front.

My mother's hands worked tirelessly on the

crown and it became a work of art when it was completed. She would take an ordinary piece of cardboard cut to fit my head and would cover it with cream-colored fabric. Glittering sequins and beads were then glued on. The final touch were the long silk ribbons, in the color of the Hungarian flag, which Mami placed at the top of the crown. The green, red and white ribbons flapped in the wind as I ice-skated around the rink in my fairy-tale dress.

My mother worked simultaneously on all the costumes. The highlight of my sister's Thai outfit was a silver, cone-shaped lamé hat. It was also covered in sequins and beads. I recognized

My sister Mona and me as Spanish prince and princess with famous Austrian actor Heinz Conrads, 1966.

crystal pieces from our chandelier on the front of the crown. Mami must have run out of beads, and to please her children and her own creative spirit, she found just what she needed from the light that hung in our dining room.

The night of the ball we walked to the *Eislaufverein* (skating rink) in our ice skates since it was too difficult to put them on in the dressing room with the heavy costumes. It was also part of the fun and tradition of every year. Red lipstick was the only makeup we had on. I was afraid to lick off the precious color and so I smiled a fake kind of smirk.

When we walked in we saw that an area was roped off for the ball, and the jury was sitting in a reserved section of the stands, placed with a bird's-eye view of the arena. Children wore all kinds of colorful costumes. I watched the clowns, penguins, bears, Little Red Riding Hoods, cowboys and Indians glide by. It was always a magical moment when we saw our mother in the gallery where she stood smiling down at us while we skated our big circles on the ice in front of the jury.

Everyone had to skate in a large circle for about half an hour until the jury made their decision on whose costumes showed the most beauty and creativity. My mother told us to smile when we passed the jury, to get their attention. My gloved hand would reach out for Tomi's and we skated side by side. After only a few minutes the jury signaled to my cousin and sister, the Thai prince and princess, to leave the circle and wait in a separate area. Not long after, my brother and I were picked out, too.

I looked up at my mother and beamed with pride. She gave us the biggest smile of encouragement and we knew that she truly felt that we were royalty.

Heinz Conrads, a famous Austrian actor, handed us the prize. Journalists were present and the TV cameramen captured the special moment. We had won again, just as we did every year until I was thirteen. That was when we decided we had to move on and let the younger children of the town take our coveted place. This year we each received a check for twenty dollars and a tray full of prizes. Small transistor radios, chocolate candies, records and a paint set were only a few of the goodies we received. The next day our pictures were printed in the local paper and glimpses of us were flashed in the news.

My mother sat among the audience watching us throughout the ceremony, giving us encouraging smiles. She wore a warm winter coat and a beaver hat pulled over her ears. If she spent time outside in the bitter cold, deep holes would appear on her skin that would only go away when she was warm again. But nothing in the world could make her miss these important moments of our lives. Nothing gave her more pleasure than to see us in her fabulous creations. She waved her hands at us and in her mind she was already planning what we would wear the next year for the Carnival on Ice.

Those were the golden moments in my life. Through Carnival on Ice Mami let us know that as a child and young girl she had lived a secure life filled with beauty and love. We knew there was another part of her past as well, because sometimes she would give us a glimpse into the darkness that had befallen her. It had only been a few years since the war, but she let none of that destroy her love, splendor and taste for magnificence. It seems ironic that these balls were in winter; many would think that the anticipation of blizzards, frozen streams and frosty trees would sadden a child, but for us it was different. We had Carnival on Ice. The severe winter was transformed into a time of light and joy as Mami provided warmth and tenderness with her magical creations.

10. *A Graduation from the Shtetl*

I was in the midst of baking *challot* for *Shabbat* when my husband called me on his cell phone from New York City, just a few seconds before our son's name was announced to receive his diploma in international law. I heard the distant loud voice announce, "Tzvika Nissel."

I started to cry. In my mind I saw him walking confidently in big strides up to the podium to receive the glossy paper which joined the rest of his diplomas on the wall.

I did not make it to New York for his graduation; my husband tried to calm me down but I was still distraught. "Mami, you've been there, done that, how many of these boring things do you want to attend. It's really not a big deal," Tzvika said as he tried to comfort me after graduating.

"It will always be a big deal for me," I said, struggling to make him understand. I distinctly remember the first time Tzvika handed me a bundle of bright blue cloth. "Mami, you have to press my gown for tomorrow," he said. I held it up to figure out what it was and quickly decided it looked like a tent. He was going to wear what our family now calls a "tent-dress."

With each and every graduation my parents, who did not have the same opportunities, graduate with my children. My father was born in a shtetl in a little town in Romania called Targu Mures and then moved to Cluj. There he went to *cheder* — traditional Jewish elementary school — until he became a teenager and attended a yeshiva in Krasna.

"It was bitter cold and still dark outside when I had to walk through the snow to yeshiva every day. My gloveless hands froze without any protection. When we got to school it wasn't any better so we sat all day long, learning Talmud, still in our overcoats."

He spent his days learning what was important to his family, keeping the tradition intact and following the footsteps of his ancestors. But then the war broke out and Talmud learning came to an abrupt halt.

Despite being cut short, their experiences in school planted deep seeds in my parents regarding the importance of education and so they made sure to send us to school.

"You have to complete *Matura*," my mother would always say to me as a little girl. These were the final exams taken at the end of secondary school which enable passing candidates to go on to university. She imagined that by sending me to the best school, *Gymnasium*, the doors of the world would be wide open for me.

I did receive a diploma of *Matura*, however my school career ended there as I got married at twenty and soon become a full-time mother to my three sons. It was 1988 when I received my first invitation to a graduation. My eldest son, Tzvika, was finishing elementary school.

The ceremony for this event took place in the local synagogue near the school. Every family member was equipped with cameras and plenty of emotion. I had no idea what to expect. But then, I heard the music. It was a familiar tune, the soundtrack to *Rocky*, one my son frequently played on the piano. It brought back a rush of memories.

I had not noticed that the program handed to me at the entrance was slowly disintegrating in my moist hands, and by the time I sat down the black ink was smudged. The principal and the teachers all gave speeches congratulating the students. Their words echoed my mother's and I realized that I, too, was devoted to making sure my sons would go as far as they could. I wanted them to graduate for themselves, for me and for their grandparents.

They too wanted to prove to their grandfather, a man who grew up in a shtetl, that only two generations later it is possible to reach for the sky and walk up to that podium one stride at a time. Out of commitment to themselves, and from a lifelong obligation to their family, they strive for continued excellence. And my father, my mother and I all graduate with them.

"Don't be upset, Mami, next year I am going to apply for the PhD program and you will have another chance to press one of those tent-dresses!"

11. *Rosemary Chocolate*

Last year I left a few items, like the chocolates and cheeses, for last-minute shopping.

"Shlomo, I need a shopping cart," I said to the nice worker I knew from my habitual shopping at this store.

"Wait here — I will go out to the street and look for one," he said.

I decided to throw myself into the mass of people and not wait for Shlomo. Equipped with a red and blue plastic hand basket I started my shopping experience a day before one of the most celebrated Jewish holidays in the calendar, Passover. I stood in front of the shelves, which seemed to curve downwards from the heavy load of different candy bars that are available today.

"Yes, Rosemary chocolate is still available even today," I thought as I placed five of them into the red basket. The sheer variety of choices left me breathless. Switzerland was still in the lead with their fine quality chocolates, but Israel and the United States had some good examples on the shelves too. I stacked a couple of boxes of almond raisin bark, presented very elegantly in a blue and gold paper with a picture of the New York skyline on it, into the basket. Thinking of my eldest son and his affinity for white chocolate, I added the Krachnuss milk and dark variety to my collection. As I stood in front of the shelves I couldn't help but reminisce about my childhood.

"Nussi, don't forget the chocolate when you go over to Zimmerman's!" my mother would yell down the staircase of our apartment building as my father descended to help with the Passover shopping.

Just anticipating eating the candy made my mouth water. My father would return from the kosher market a few hours later. If we were lucky the silver metal can was filled to the rim with fresh milk. But at times when Papa was not one of the first ones in line for milk he would come back without it and we could not enjoy our favorite drink during this holiday: cocoa with soaked matza. Most of the time he brought home milk and a shopping bag full of items such as: matza meal, sugar, salt, pepper and eggs. But the most important item was the Rosemary chocolate. He always bought us our treat.

Nothing gave us more pleasure than when my older sister Mona would call out, "Rosemary time!" We would gather around her on the pink velvet sofa, full of excitement. If I listen closely I can still hear the rustling of the silver foil being peeled back to reveal the brown color of our favorite treat. The outer wrapping was brown and green, a beautiful, warm, inviting green that welcomed us children sweetly into the days of saltwater and bitter horseradish. For a split moment in time all we could think about was how to make the tiny piece of candy last for a long time.

Mona would take one rectangle piece and equally divide it into thirds. Mona cut the chocolate with mathematical precision. We stared at her wide-eyed and eager to accept what she handed to us. Then came the instructions: "Don't bite it, Rebecca and Tomi, you have to indulge. It will disappear in a zip if you bite. Place a tiny bit on your tongue, like a sucking candy."

I placed the piece between my pointer and thumb, but for just a second so that it would not melt from my excited sweaty fingers, and then I did as my older and wiser sister instructed. I leaned back against the sofa, closed my eyes and was sure that I was in heaven. Whoever succeeded in keeping the tiny treasure on their tongue for the longest time would be the winner. Every couple of minutes we would open our mouths and reveal the brown gooey mass that was once Rosemary chocolate, and then we would continue with our sweet dreams. At times Mona was frivolous and shared a second rectangular piece with us, but then we knew that bar would not last for the entire eight days of Passover.

A lady bumped into me and startled me back into reality as I stood in front of the chocolate shelf. Slowly, I pushed my way to the selection of cheeses in the refrigerator section. My husband happened to have been on a low-carbohydrate diet around that time so besides all the candy treats, I needed to buy a large quantity of cheeses for snacks. I was almost trampled to death trying to reach the glass cases that held hundreds of different Kosher for Passover dairy products. I placed the red basket filled with the candy in the corner behind some wire shelves that held eggs and other very important ingredients for the holidays. The second basket, which I intended to fill with cheeses, I put right next to it since it was impossible to squeeze through the masses of people holding anything in front of me. I went back and forth between my hidden basket and the fridge, dropping packages of Emmenthaler, Munster and American cheese inside. The selection of Israeli, French and Swiss cheeses was incredible. Everything that was available during the year somehow was also permitted to eat during the sacred holiday of Passover.

Cheese was almost nonexistent when I was growing up in Vienna and if we did find it, it was too expensive for us to buy. Only much later, when I had my first paying job in the Lander Bank, would I enter the premises of Zimmerman Kosher Grocery to buy a package of individually sliced cheese. For lunch I would buy a fresh roll and place one of the cheese slices between the bread. That's what I considered enjoying cheese.

"Could I just reach for some cheddar cheese?" said a lady as she used my already bruised shoulder as a fortification to reach into the fridge.

"Thank you," she said and disappeared into the dark crowd of shoppers.

I returned to the shelf of eggs behind which I had hidden my two baskets only to realize that one was missing. I searched in vain; my candy basket was gone. With tired, weary eyes I looked at the long lines of people in front of the cashiers.

"Maybe World War III is breaking out," I thought.

I decided it was enough shopping for one day. The basket with cheeses heaped to the rim was left in the corner behind the eggs. I told Albert, one of the storeowners, to tell somebody to return them to the fridge. As I ran out of the store I passed stacks of large Coca-Cola bottles with the Kosher for Passover stamped yellow tops.

"Tomorrow I'll buy the Coke," I thought, and

hoped that they would not run out of the sweet drink before the next day.

I found my car four blocks down the street and sank into the comfortable leather upholstery exhausted from my shopping experience.

"Let's cut the chocolate piece into equal little triangles," my sister Mona suggested one year.

"Good idea," I said.

With the taste of Rosemary chocolate in my mouth I drove towards home with not one item purchased, but with many fond memories of Passover in my heart.

12. *Goal*

Years ago, when I was six years old, Papa started taking us to the *Fussballmatch* (soccer game). We — my sister, my brother and I — did not even think about any other Sunday plans. Attending soccer games became a routine like my mother's laundry.

My mother never got hooked on the game. "I don't understand," she often said, "why people get so excited watching a group of men chase after a ball."

Papa did not even bother explaining. He was just happy that we understood and went along with him. We had breakfast in the morning, packed a snack and off we were to the *Stadion*. We rooted for Austria-Wien, die Violetten (the Purple Ones).

Sometimes Papa felt sorry for the children of his friends whose fathers did not care for *Fussball*, so he took them with him. These boys were forever grateful to my father. They loved him. Today he would be considered "cool."

Even though polite children addressed grown-ups with Herr or Frau, Papa was on a first name basis with all of them. They used to say, "Nussi, can we buy a drink?" or, "Nussi, can we get peanuts?"

Papa was their friend and he was proud of those friendships. I can visualize us all on the tram now, crowding around him and cracking jokes, a little nervous in anticipation of the game.

In a way, we took these weekly rides to the *Stadion* for granted. For some of these little friends, however, it was the first time and they were thrilled. The tram conductor announced: "*Endstation, Wiener Stadion, alles aussteigen*! (Final stop, Vienna Stadium, everybody out!)" And we hurried off the tram to reach the entrance to the gate on time.

After passing the person who checked our tickets, we ran to our seats. Sometimes we made up little songs while we sat on the wooden seats. We sang in a chorus, "*Austria vor, noch ein Tor!* (Go Austria, another goal!)"

The big moment, a goal, was like magic. All our anxiety, anticipation, angst, everything was let out in that scream. "*Tooooor!* (Goal!)"

We sang, clapped our hands, and hugged each other and we loved it. The emotion we displayed was of a magnitude I would probably reserve today for news like the engagement of one of my sons!

Oh my, how times have changed!

Those first encounters with the world of

Fussball in the company of our father were very special. We received our first television set in 1966 in honor of the World Cup. Everything revolved around those games. Homework was completed in the minimal amount of time and we never prepared for any tests. My parents' store closed for lunch for almost two hours, even though it had no scheduled lunch hour. Piano and ballet lessons were canceled due to terrible "headaches." Our world stood still while we watched those athletes from all over the world "chase the ball."

Recently, my world came to a halt when I decided to watch the game on the Spanish-speaking channel. My shopping for *Shabbat* was postponed until the next day. The paying of the bills could be done in the evening and I remembered that I still had delicious leftover lasagna from last week for dinner. Alone in my bedroom, I switched on the TV in anticipation of the game. It was not the same. Something was missing and I knew what I wanted to do. I called my father long-distance to Vienna. Once I heard his voice, it felt like old times.

"Mona, is it you?" he asked.

"No, Papa, it's your daughter in California."

"Maybe I should root for Cameroon and forget about those Nazi Austrians. No, I can't do that. I am an Austrian for too long."

"Papa, it's okay to root for Austria. I do, too."

We continued to talk for a while and I finally

put down the receiver, realizing that long-distance for an hour and a half would be too costly. I watched the game on my own. Cameroon scored in the second half and then Austria tied the game. The announcer on the Spanish channel screamed, "Goooooooal!"

And in my excitement, I called Papa again and we watched the repeat of the goal together.

"Beautiful goal, a decisive goal!" my father yelled into the phone.

It sounded like the old days when he was thrilled that his favorite team had succeeded.

I was thousands of miles away, but at that moment I felt so close.

13. *Fun Vonent Kumt a Yid*

My father and I walked on 13th Avenue in Boro
Park, Brooklyn. Our destination was the bookstore called Eichlers where my father wanted to
buy some Judaica for his local synagogue in
Vienna. Boro Park reminds me of the movie
Hester Street, the hustle and bustle of Jews on the
streets and in the stores. There were pregnant
women with as many as three babies in carriages, a toddler on each arm and maybe
another one clinging to the mother's coat walking behind her legs.

"You see this man over there by the cashier
in the grocery, I bet you he is from Satu Mare
(Satmar) or that area."

I looked at the man, who was maybe in his
late seventies. He wore a gray hat that was
pulled down low onto his forehead. His wrin-
kled face showed only eyes, the rest disappeared
with age.

"How can you tell, Papa?" I asked.

"Well, I can't identify him for sure, but I am
almost positive so I am going over to ask him."

He approached the man, who was just about

to walk away from the store. *"Fun vonent kumt a Yid?* (Where are you from?)" he inquired.

The stranger looked at my father, and within a few seconds they had struck up a conversation. It was incredible to watch how they got involved in a deep discussion without any apparent previous contact.

"Rebecca, come over here, I have to introduce you to Mr. Jabotinsky, he is from Siebenburgen, just like me. This is my daughter, she lives in California."

At one point, when we all seemed to become related to one another (I felt the bloodline begin to flow), I pulled my father's coat and whispered into his ear that we had to go.

We continued on our way, my father all the while explaining and telling stories. We stopped frequently as he would turn to me and use his hands to emphasize a point he wanted me to understand. After a few seconds we continued to walk. This was a habit of his which made keeping to a schedule impossible. The walk to Eichlers normally takes me ten minutes; with my father meeting new relatives en route and telling stories, we hadn't the slightest hope of reaching our destination.

"Maybe I should get a new shirt for the wedding of Avromi?" my father asked.

We stepped into a small store, which looked like it had not been remodeled since the 1950s, but was neat and organized. Behind the counter stood a white-bearded gentleman with a black vest who was waiting on two customers. They were paying him for two white shirts that they were already holding in their hands.

My father approached the elderly man.

"I know your uncle Duvid who lived in Vienna. I still live there." And with that, another long dialogue started.

Here we were, in this dress shirt shop, and my father completely forgot the purpose for which we were there. He was engrossed in a discourse with Duvid's nephew. The other customers waited in line, listening in on the conversation, held in Yiddish. After a few minutes, they too, were involved in the talk and I felt the bloodline running again, between everybody around me.

"We need a nice white shirt for my father for the wedding of his grandchild," I blurted out.

"Itzik, where are you, bring the $17 shirt for my friend here. We have to sell him the better kind. He is making a *chasseneh* (wedding)."

I had not even noticed Itzik, who appeared from behind neatly stacked up brown boxes containing shirts. He ran his finger up the stack, pulled out the box and presented to us the better shirt. I did not even have to look at it. From the corner of my eye I stared at Itzik, whose shirt was yellow from overuse and the collar sprinkled with tiny holes. The zipper of his trousers was held together with a couple of safety pins. He handed me the better shirt with an almost toothless grin.

"Do you think I can have the top-of-the-line $35 shirt with the French Cuffs?" I asked him.

Itzik shuffled back to the shelf, carrying his age on his bent shoulders. He removed another box and appeared with the "top-of-the-line" in his hands. The men were still engrossed in their conversation. They were talking about the old times back in Romania. The only thing that was missing was the aroma of brewing black coffee. My father still visits his favorite coffee shop every day in Vienna where he meets up with his friends. At this point, these men were his friends too.

We left the store with the wedding shirt tucked into a plastic shopping bag. We passed Gold's hat store and then stopped at Pizza Delight.

"Are you hungry, Rebecca?" my father asked me.

"I could eat a slice of eggplant pizza," I said.

We entered the shop and stood in front of the counter to wait our turn to order.

"*Fun vonent kumt a Yid?*" I heard the familiar words next to me. My father was at it again.

After many months of recovery and rehabilitation from the four different concentration camps my father survived, the first thing he did was to look for his family. He received a train pass and traveled from camp to camp to read the survivor list posted on the wall at each one of them. Maybe my father is still searching for his lost friends and relatives. Maybe he is connecting himself to his childhood, searching the streets of 13th Avenue for his beloved people, who might take the shape of strangers in whose eyes he can read the affirmation: "I understand; I know where you come from."

When we left after our pizza lunch with the "new relative," we headed back to the apartment. Of course we never made it to Eichlers bookstore.

14.   *The Promise*

Tailfingen, another not so well known camp, was the third concentration camp my father was transported to in cattle cars. Tailfingen reminded the inmates of the German word *Teufel*, meaning the devil. "We certainly had a devilish time in this place," my father said. I once asked him how much time he had spent in Tailfingen before he was transported to the "hospital" at Vaihingen-Enz. He told me he really didn't know exactly — "six weeks, seven weeks, eight weeks, I had no concept of time, because it was a minute to minute survival."

It was still a bitter snowy winter. Apparently here they didn't need the inmates to do any productive work — or perhaps they were simply too weak to produce anything — but at any rate the Nazis invented work for them. A huge mountain of sand was assembled in one place and then my father was whipped into shoveling the sand from the huge pile onto another place nearby, for no reason other than to engage him in hard labor. At one point he decided not to continue this nonsense torture and checked into the infirmary. There he was left to die. He survived by shoveling dirt and eating coals.

In the infirmary, Papa met another man from his hometown, Mr. Klein, who had become too sick to do anything. Mr. Klein was older than my father and he knew he wouldn't survive. My father was close to him and tended to him as much as he could. Before he died he called my father over to his bed.

"Nussikam, you will make it out of here. Please promise me you will tell my sons where I died so that they can say Kaddish at my grave." My father promised, helpless to do anything else for his older friend. He took careful note of where they buried Mr. Klein.

After the war, in addition to searching for survivors from our own family, Papa was always trying to locate one of Mr. Klein's sons. But it was only years later, in the sixties, that a tall, handsome gentleman who spoke Hungarian walked into our store in Vienna. "Nussi, is it you?" the man said. My father recognized the distinguished features of the Klein family and immediately reached out his arms to hug this young stranger. Mr. Klein's son was a diplomat in Bucharest, Romania and did a lot of traveling; Papa was so grateful that the young man's appearance in his store allowed him to keep his promise. He drew a map of the camp in Tailfingen and marked the site where Mr. Klein's father was buried in a mass grave.

A promise made to a person who was dying under the most horrific conditions was a task for life; a task to find somebody and convey an important message. It was a sacred trust. Sometimes these promises were the only way for family members to know for certain what had become of their loved ones. And sometimes a promise was in answer to the plea in a doomed person's eyes: "Remember me, don't let me be forgotten."

My father made such a promise to Gyula Baci, a man he had known as a customer of his family's bakery back home. They were acquaintances, but nothing more. However in the camps Gyula became a fellow Jew.

One night, standing next to my father in the cold rain of Auschwitz, Gyula's number was called during *Zählappel*. They stood together in their thin pajamas. He was called by his number and he knew that he would die within the next half an hour.

Gyula Baci turned to my father and said, "Mr. Liebermann, I don't understand. I did not even know I was Jewish before the Nazis took me, and now I am going to die."

"Today it is you," my father answered, "but tomorrow it could be me."

As the rain poured down, Papa stood next to Gyula Baci in a muddy river, and promised never to forget him.

15. *Yizkor*

I could not keep up with my mother's fast pace and I was trailing a few steps behind her. She wore her Yizkor suit, a black skirt and jacket with sequins on the collar and a white ruffled blouse.

"I have to make it on time for Yizkor," she said as she turned around to see how far behind I was. Yizkor, from the root word meaning "remember," is the special prayer recited for a parent — or both parents — who have passed away. It is said four times a year during holiday prayers, only by people who have lost a parent; those fortunate enough to have both parents living must leave the synagogue during the prayer.

"Yizkor, Yizkor, children out," all the women would say in raised voices as we were pushed and shoved through the narrow opening of the women's section of our tiny synagogue in Grunangergasse. My mother too was anxious to get me out of the room onto the shabby wooden balcony that was open to the fresh cold air. Sometimes I forgot to take my coat or sweater during the hasty exit and stood there shivering and wondering what exactly took place during Yizkor. I always imagined that through some miracle both sets of grandparents descended from Gan Eden, to tell my parents that they were really alright and that G-d and His angels were taking good care of them. I thought my mother was so concerned about being in *shul* on time because her parents came down during Yizkor and she would actually miss them if she were late.

I imagined them floating down to earth from heaven into this holy room and embracing my parents, allowing them to feel the warmth of their father and mother for just a few moments during those few times a year. They were all so young when they died. My father told me that his mother, Toby Bat Efraim, was killed in Auschwitz on the day of deportation and his father, Shrager Zvi Ben Yehuda, died just a couple of days before Kaufering was liberated. Papa was only eighteen years old when he became an orphan. I stood outside on the balcony and wondered why it was possible to see them only four times a year. Why not a few more times? Why couldn't they come during school plays when I performed on stage in *Little Red Riding Hood*? All my gentile schoolmates brought their grandparents to sit in the audience and cheer for them at the end of the performance. Or, would it not have been nice to attend my sixth birthday, the day I proudly received my first book bag for school?

My mother still had her mother when I was little — in fact I met my maternal grandmother once on a trip to Israel when I was six years old. But a couple of years later she passed away and I never again had the comfort of knowing I had a grandparent. I never knew what it meant to have grandparents. Neither did my friends in synagogue, the ones who huddled together with me on the balcony. They too were children of survivors. Sometimes that gave me comfort. Nobody walked to *shul* holding their grandparents' hands.

At one point, maybe fifteen minutes later, usually a father would come out of the men's section and say, "Go back inside, *Kinderlach*, Yizkor is over."

I would return to my mother who always cried when I came back. As a child I knew it was not because she missed me so much in that short period of time, but because she could not stop crying after saying good-bye to her parents. It must have been so hard for her to only hug her father and mother for fifteen minutes knowing they would disappear again for the next few months. She held her white cloth hankie, with the pink rose embroidery; it looked all crinkled and wet in her hand. Everybody's mother cried when we returned. I felt like crying, too. I wanted to hug them.

Many years have passed since then and I still go out during the Yizkor prayer — my parents should live until 120. However, now I know that my grandparents did not return to embrace my parents during this special prayer. All they have are the memories, or maybe it's only a simple desire to show respect to the people who loved them most. My mother's father died when she was only two years old, yet till today she rushes to *shul* to be on time for that virtual meeting with her parents.

16. *Kaufering*

After a three-and-a-half-hour bus ride we were trudging through the wet mud. I could not stop thinking of my mother's words before we went on this trip: "Wear good shoes, because there are no paved streets in Kaufering."

Kaufering is a small village, about two hundred kilometers from Munich. Seventeen members of my extended family, including myself, were going to visit the grave of my grandfather. Typhus had stolen the last breath out of his already shriveled body a few days before liberation. There were two lone gravestones standing above a mass grave of many thousands and his was one of them.

The occasion for the family gathering was the wedding of my niece in Zurich, Switzerland. The day before the big event my sister had rented a fancy bus that would take us past the Swiss border into Germany. I was a bit confused whether I was doing the right thing or not. Would I be in the right frame of mind to visit such a sad place and then celebrate the next day, as though nothing had happened? I went. I knew I must honor my grandfather.

On the bus the anticipation of seeing my grandfather's grave made me anxious. To calm my nerves I decided to interview my aunts and uncles: my father's sisters, his brother and brother-in-law. Each one had a different story of survival to tell and I wrote while they talked. I specifically remember sitting next to my Tante Feigi. "You don't even know how special your father is," she told me.

"A few months after we were deported to Auschwitz my teeth started to fall out from mal-nutrition. Many times your father snuck into the SS warehouse and stole toothpowder for me. He would wait until no one was around and then he would throw it to me over the dividing wall between the men's and women's barracks. Once he was caught, though, and the SS officer whipped him right there in front of me. They warned him that if they ever caught him again they would kill him. I never understood how or why, but he did it again. This time the SS grabbed him. We thought that this would be it. They were going to kill him. They dragged him into a room with a low ceiling."

At that moment my father knew they were just playing a torturous game: a mock hanging. "Say your last prayer, Jew," they snickered.

The mood on the bus was somber and quiet except for the rustling of the cellophane wrap as we reached for the sandwiches my sister had prepared for the trip. Some were immersed in thought staring ahead; others talked quietly, so as not to disturb the other relatives who had fallen asleep to the rhythmic motion of the bus.

Even though my father had gone dozens of times to visit his father's grave, for some reason or other, I had never gone along with him. He never asked me to, and I guess deep down I was afraid to go. I was afraid of my emotions. I was scared of standing in a concentration camp with my father and seeing the place he had suffered so horridly in. It was too real. I was still afraid now, but there was strength in numbers as I looked around the bus at all these dear faces.

My father was the guide and instructed the bus driver where to turn to reach the village. The weather was sunny when we passed the Bodensee (Lake Constance) and almost as if in sync with our emotions it began to rain when we reached Kaufering. Most of us had protective gear: we had taken our raincoats and some of us were prepared with umbrellas. We descended from the bus with my father leading the way to his father's grave. After walking a few hundred yards through the forest we finally saw a lone gravestone partially hidden in the green.

"Papa, is this the stone?" He nodded. I walked faster and faster. For some reason I wanted to arrive at the stone first and touch it before anyone else did. I knew my father could not go all the way to his father's gravestone because he is a Cohen. A Cohen is a member of the priestly class, who performed the Temple rites during the times of the First and Second Temples. Purity laws forbid them to come in close contact with the dead even today. He stopped abruptly behind a two-foot wall and stood there while we continued on our way for another few feet.

The Hebrew letters on the gravestone were wet with the rain and my tears. The heavens cried with all of us as we stood touching my grandfather's grave. He had died *al kiddush Hashem*. I spoke aloud, telling him that there were three generations of his descendants at his grave and that we continued to live a Torah life. I reassured him, or maybe myself, that he had not lost his life in vain. We asked him for a blessing for my niece who was getting married the next day. I told him that I was grateful for my father, his son, who survived to raise us as a family. I told him that he died in order for us to exist in this world, free of persecution, free from fear of existence, and with a Jewish state of our own.

My aunts hugged the stone and cried.

The entire family recited *Tehillim* (Psalms) together. Then my father and my Uncle Czumi, who still stood behind the low wall, a few feet away, said *Kel Malei Rachamim* ("G-d full of mercy," a prayer for the dead). When they completed their prayers my father said, "Somebody decided that this is where the mass grave ends, but, does it really? I think that right now at this very moment I am standing on holy ground. This is holy earth."

I wanted to float instead of walk, so as not to desecrate the place. My shoes sank into the mud as I walked to a nearby memorial. It had been erected a few years after the war for the many Jewish victims buried in haste in this mass grave.

I wondered why my grandfather had a gravestone and so many other victims did not. My father told me that a few weeks before the liberation the Germans became careless about the comings and goings of prisoners. They themselves were aware of the fact that the war was almost over. Intense bombing by Allied troops could be heard almost twenty-four hours around the clock. It was Mr. Perlmutter, a friend from my father's town, who had buried my grandfather. He had marked the place clearly with rocks and a sign with his name. Mr. Perlmutter met my father a year after the war in Cluj, their hometown, and together they traveled to Kaufering where my father set the stone in a matter of a few days.

It had been an important act for him, placing that gravestone on his father's grave. "Seeing and touching this gravestone gives me closure," my father said. "For me this single large stone represents both my father's and my mother's grave because here I can touch. It is something tangible."

It was still raining when we boarded the bus. I felt a need to stay longer in this place. I didn't want to leave my grandfather's side. But I knew that it was not possible; soon it would get dark and the family had to return to Zurich to get ready for the wedding the next day.

Everybody was quiet on the bus, busy with their own thoughts. I held out my hand almost like I wanted to physically take my grandfather with me from the burial place in the forest in Kaufering to Zurich to the wedding of his great-granddaughter. I tried to connect with him in mind and spirit and at that moment I knew that it was the right thing to honor my grandfather the day before the wedding. All my previous doubts and fears of what kind of effect it could have were calmed down. It was like the age-old tradition of the groom who breaks the glass under the *chuppa* (bridal canopy) to remember the destruction of the Holy Temple; even in celebration we always remember our loss and that our joy is not complete until the Temple stands again.

And so we remembered our grandfather during this time, and our grandmother and all the other family members who perished, and we took them along on the bus to Zurich, almost a real physical presence.

The next day at my niece's beautiful *chuppa* I blinked my eyes twice and I thought I saw my grandfather holding onto my father's hand. He smiled at me, the same kind of smile he wears in the photograph on the mantel in my living room.

17. The Power of a Voice

Once in a while he tried to communicate with the friendly voices that surrounded him, but the people who seemed very concerned and friendly talked in a language he did not understand. With pity in their eyes the friendly soldiers in unfamiliar uniforms tried to convey a message to my father. The only thing he understood was that he was free and that the language he did not comprehend was French. Thoughts ran through his mind: "It's over, it's over. Auschwitz, Stutthof and Tailfingen. And only now in Vaihingen-Enz do the gates of freedom open." With his last bit of strength he sang *"La Marseillaise"* (the French national anthem) and it brought tears to the eyes of the French liberators.

Singing was always the best way of communicating for my father. Often the deepest feelings come forth through something creative. Some paint, others write and some, like my father, sing. When he serves as the *chazzan* (cantor) of his synagogue on High Holidays, congregants can't help but cry when they hear him. His voice trembles with emotion as he recognizes that he is not only the *chazzan* but, as a Cohen, he carries the responsibility of representing the entire congregation before G-d.

"My voice gets better the older I get," he said to me on my last trip to Vienna. We had been walking for about two miles towards our apartment in the inner city when my father mentioned this to me. At that moment, trudging through deep snow, icy wind blowing, I could only think about my father's red ears protruding from underneath his *Shabbat* hat. I constantly told him to stop walking, so that I could tie the white cashmere shawl around his face and ears a bit tighter; it kept slipping down and made me worry that he would catch a cold.

"It was easy to sing in that *shul*, Rebecca, the acoustics are great. I didn't strain my voice at all." The *gabbai* of the Tempelgasse Synagogue, the one who arranges all the details of the prayer services, loved when my father made the extra long walk to this *shul* on special *simchas* (celebrations) and took every opportunity to have him sing in front of the congregants. After this particular *Shabbat* one of the members of the *shul* called and said, "I don't know what it is, but something in your voice makes me feel so much closer to G-d." When I heard this, I finally realized how lucky I was to have grown up surrounded by my father's voice.

When I think of our *Shabbat* table as a little

girl, I remember how we sang more than we talked. Our conversations started and ended with *zemirot*, the traditional *Shabbat* songs. Singing in our home began with the tunes my father hummed to himself when he returned from *shul* and they continued with the *zemirot* that we sang during and after the meal. He often would say, "My children, learn this, learn this one. This is from your grandfather." Then he would continue to repeat the song over and over until we finally got it. My mother, on the other hand, was the best critique of our choir. She would immediately interrupt us when we were a little off tune, saying, "Stop it, stop it, wrong tune… wrong tune," and we had to begin again. My older sister Mona, younger brother Tomi and I could hold a tune pretty well, and it had become such a routine for us that we all knew that in the future we would have to marry someone who could sing.

Every year, during the High Holidays of Rosh Hashanah and Yom Kippur, my father would rent out a beautiful building on the waterways of the *Stadtpark*, and move hundreds of people with his voice during these days of repentance. I remember, not long after the war, how the loud crying voices of the congregation accompanied my father's powerful voice. It was mostly the survivors who expressed their pain and suffering with loud cries of anguish. I asked him after the services, "Papa, doesn't it interrupt you, all that screaming and crying?"

His answer carried much power. "Interrupt me? No, I am the *shaliach tzibur*, the representative of the congregation, and the crying voices are a constant reminder of that." As one of the last living survivors of the Holocaust, the importance he places on his task as *chazzan* has grown throughout the years. It hit me after he recently awoke from an eight-hour colon cancer surgery. The first thing he said to me was, "Do you think my voice will be strong enough in just two months to sing on the High Holidays?" This is who my father is: a man who gains strength, even when he has none at all, through his strong belief in G-d. The G-d who gave him the unique voice to thank his liberators in song.

18. *Chariots of Fire*

I spotted them from afar, pacing around the corner; all of them together like a cluster of grapes on a vine. I had been doubtful that I would ever find them; my son only told me, "Go to Hollywood Park at three o'clock and you will see us." He was right; I saw them right away. How could I have thought that I would miss a group of boys in black and white uniform with *kippot* (skullcaps) on their heads?

Hundreds of young people from many different prestigious high schools had gathered with their coaches in the park to prepare for the big race. My son and the other kids from his Orthodox Jewish high school, YULA, were huddled together listening to their coach's last minute advice. At one point, one of the team members led some pre-game warm-ups. Another was helping his friend stand up, while another was handing a bottle of water to the kid next to him. They all were leaning on each other for support. A group of boys, maybe four or five, placed one hand against a large tree and stretched their legs. As I snapped pictures with my camera, they were completely oblivious to my doings.

Coach Ablin took the older group, the varsity team, for a last minute short warm-up jog and then they were ready. The YULA kids took their position in the middle of the crowd of kids. As they assembled they loudly chanted, "YULA, YULA, YULA," and lined up one behind another. I quickly walked across the park; I wanted to spot them on the other side and mimic their encouraging yells of "GO YULA." As I watched them run by with sweat dripping down their necks, I could see that they were intensely focused on their final goal, the finish line. YULA's varsity team came in first.

My son, Erez, ran in the junior varsity team and it was their turn a little while after. I was more nervous than Erez, who looked very calm. His team also rounded up and shouted "YULA" before the starting line. I jogged back and forth across the racetrack, trying to spot them so I could cheer them on. I must have covered three miles.

As a teenager, growing up in Vienna, Austria, I ran a lot. Not because I participated in races like my sons did, but because I was scared. I thought that I had to be able to outrun every Nazi in the city of Vienna. I convinced myself that anyone around me could be dangerous: the conductor of the tram asking for my ticket, or even the policeman who regulated traffic at the street corner. I became the fastest sprinter in my class.

I stopped running when I first visited Israel in 1969, when I was fifteen years old. I felt safe among my fellow Jews and I found a calmness and peacefulness in my soul. Even when I returned to my hometown to resume school I didn't feel the urge to run anymore. I thought of my Jewish homeland, only a three-hour flight from Vienna, and it gave me stability of mind.

When I watched my son's schoolmates running, surrounded by hundreds of other kids from different schools, I finally understood what it meant to run as a team. I remember asking my son, when he was already at the starting line, "Erez, do you need two pins to secure your *kippa?*" He shook his head, he did not need any pins; he and the other kids wore them firmly on their heads. They did not feel the loneliness of being Jewish, like I did as a child. They did not run because they wanted to outrun an anti-Semite. They ran with pride for their school and for who they were.

As they crossed the finish line each boy got a pat on the shoulder and words of praise from their coaches: "You did great. You really picked up speed at the end." But more than that, the boys felt that they were part of a greater team, and they were united on a deeper level, regardless of who came in first or last.

The last words I heard from the coach before

they headed back on the bus made me realize once again how different life is now. "Don't forget to clean up the orange peels and collect the water bottles from the ground," he told them. "We don't want to make a *chillul Hashem* (to make people think, G-d forbid, that those who observe G-d's Torah do not behave properly)."

19. *Role Change*

A red light at the corner of Olympic Boulevard and Beverly Drive made me come to an abrupt stop. An elderly gentleman, maybe seventy-five years or older, dressed in a beige cap — the kind my father wears in the summertime — and a gray rain jacket with a zipper, held the hand of a man who I assumed was his son. The younger man wore a red baseball cap, a plaid shirt, khaki pants and the same jacket as the father, but in a darker shade. Both of them stood still at the curb waiting for the signal to change. I noticed that the younger man showed features of mental illness in his facial expressions. I stood in the first row of waiting cars as the two men walked right in front of my windshield, only a few feet away.

Both stared ahead, neither talking; they were engulfed in their thoughts, or maybe thinking of nothing at all except crossing the long street ahead of them. Their synchronized pace, slow and monotonous, seemed to confirm my assumption that they were indeed father and son.

Who held whose hand for protection? Did the elderly man squeeze his son's hand for support? Or did the younger man hold onto his father in fear that he would be left alone in this mad world? How could he find Pavilions supermarket on his own? Cars and trucks raced past them on every side, not paying any attention to the men's existence.

Cars started to beep their horns at me; obviously I did not budge from my spot. The only thing I felt were the warm tears trickling down my cheeks, as I watched the image of the two men disappear on the other side of Beverly Drive. I was on my way to pick up my youngest son, Erez, from school and now I would be late. I should have left two minutes earlier and then I would have made the green light and he would not have to wait for me outside in the cold.

The image of father and son struck me. Impulsively I fished out my cell phone and called my parents long-distance to Vienna. My father picked up the phone.

"How was your day, Papa?" I asked.

"Good, I just came home from *shul* and now we are getting ready to have a little dinner."

His voice sounded good. I have learned how much my parents' voices can reveal through the wires. I felt a sudden pang, a longing to be there to take care of them.

I clearly remember when for the first time I felt that instead of me taking care of my children, the roles were reversed and one of them was taking care of me. It was about ten years ago, when I was on a trip to London visiting my middle son Chaimi, who attended the University of London for three years.

From the moment I landed Chaimi took control. He had arranged for a taxi to pick me up and take me to town. After I entered his house, through the back sliding door, I plopped myself on a comfortable sofa to relax. As I stared at the coffee table I recognized my son's handwriting on a little notepad. He had left me instructions:

> *Welcome to London, Mami. Following are a few things you could do if you are not too tired. If you want to sleep, go upstairs — my bed has fresh linen. I will sleep on the sofa downstairs during your stay. If you feel like sightseeing, then head to town with the Tube (subway) or a taxi. Here are the numbers you could call. Don't take a taxi on the street; they are more expensive and only for stupid tourists who enjoy riding in the old-fashioned vehicles.*
>
> *Have a good day; see you after school around 6 P.M.*

I was not sure what I wanted to do at this point except to take a shower. I headed to the second floor in search of my son's bedroom. I did not know which one of the three bedrooms was my son's. Then I saw the yellow Post-it with an arrow pointing to the right. On it were the words, "my room." In his bathroom I found more yellow Post-it stickers. "Sorry, Mami, the faucet for hot water is broken. Be careful — it could fall off if you turn it too much to the left."

Then I found another sticker next to the shower curtain. "Place the curtain inside the tub, so the floor will not be flooded." I noticed fresh towels on a small chair, which he had prepared for me.

I felt refreshed after showering but decided that I did not have enough strength to take the Tube into town. Instead I figured I would walk in the city of Golders Green and get my circulation going.

On the front door a Post-it: "Mami, don't forget when you cross the street, first look right and then left, it's exactly the opposite from in America. Don't forget!"

Throughout my one-week stay, I felt like Chaimi, who was only twenty years old then, had switched into protective mode. He could sense when I was tired from a whole day of sightseeing and would suggest that I stay home and order in dinner. On *Shabbat* when we left the house to walk to *shul*, he saw me in my fur coat and thought it would not be a good idea to wear fur in England because of the animal rights activists who throw paint on people wearing fur.

"I did not bring another winter coat along."

"That's okay, Mami, you could wear mine and I will use the lined raincoat."

He showed me London by night, took me to nice restaurants, and made sure that while he was at university, my day was planned in advance full of pleasant highlights.

The week went by quickly and I left to the airport too soon.

"What has just happened?" I asked myself in the taxi.

For the first time in my life the roles were reversed. Yes, I was still a mother and the kids would always come home, and I would cook and bake and do all the things that they loved. But did they still need me as much anymore?

That's when I realized that the people I needed to support most now and talk to more frequently were my parents. On my next trip to Vienna, as I always do, I held my father's hand when we walked to *shul* together. This time, however, it was not just because I love doing it. Part of me wanted to protect him and prevent him from tripping, and I think I also wanted to sense the special warmth I felt as a little girl. But then he looked to the left and to the right before crossing the street to make sure his daughter was protected from the rushing traffic of oncoming cars.

"What took you so long, Mami?" Erez always asks me the same question when I pick him up late from school. But then he noticed my silence and that my usual perkiness and questions about his day were absent.

"How come you don't ask me how school was?" he asked encouragingly.

I began to tell him about the image I had just seen. He smiled and jokingly said, "Mami, are you crying because you are afraid that when you are old I will stick you into an old-age home and whenever I come to visit you I will be late and you will ask, what took you so long?"

20. *Tree of Life*

The wedding date is June 9, but the needlepoint lady told me she needs about two to three weeks for the sewing of the velvet bag. I stitched about five rows of the blue background color in one hour. The flowers are all in bloom. The blue wisteria droops her dark and light blue blossoms, as does the pink jasmine. My favorite is definitely the dahlia. I stitched it in three shades of purple and it looks quite real. The bark of the tree is completed. I had fun with it; I did it in three shades of brown. I began my project with the darkest brown of the tree trunk and when the branches started to bend around the curve, I was disoriented and made lots of mistakes. I opened those first stitches and redid the dark brown trunk. Now, I am stuck at the hardest part of my *tallit* bag, the background color.

I have till the end of May to complete my son's bag. I *schlep* my needlepoint with me wherever I go. Today at the car wash I did two rows of blue while waiting for my car to be wiped clean. People walked by me and admired my work. I realize that I can do two things while stitching. If I am not on the phone or watching the news, I think as I work my needle. Sometimes, I cry, because I cannot imagine that in just seven weeks my son will stand under the *chuppa* and wear his *tallit* the next morning. I watch my tree grow and blossom and think about the tree I saw just three years ago in Kaufering.

I see the white stone rising out of the bleak ground as I think back to my first trip to my grandfather's grave. There were only two gravestones in the cemetery. One belonged to my grandfather and the other was a bit of a mystery. There were no words of explanation on it except a simple etching of a tree with a few lines underneath listing the murdered family members. It was a traditional tree with many branches, all of them severed (pointing towards or touching the ground), except one bough that reached up to *shamayim*, heaven. It was my sister-in-law Miriam, Tomi's wife, who pointed out its meaning to me. I had first only read the lines without realizing its powerful symbolism. There had been only one survivor of this family and it was he who erected this gravestone. He was the sole survivor. He was the single branch that reached up to the heavens, the one who would continue the next generation, the symbol of hope and a continuance of life.

My father, too, was one of the few boughs in

his family tree that was able to continue to bear fruit after its branches had been so cruelly severed. I celebrate my grandfather as the real cause for my father's survival; Papa had the strength and the will to live because my grandfather planted it in him. I knew this from the stories my father had told me, and particularly from one incident which happened immediately after they arrived together in Auschwitz-Birkenau.

My grandfather, my father and his brother-in-law Yankl were still together then, just after arrival, crammed into a bunk. Another brother-in-law, Chaim, was in another bunk. They were exhausted and traumatized from their rough train ride. The only food the Nazis would throw to them was "Blutwurst," which was pork sausage.

My grandfather, a Chassidic Jew, held up the sausage for his son to see clearly what he was about to do. He looked my father in the eyes and he told him, "*Ess, ess mein Kind, die misst haben Koach* (Eat, eat my child, you have to have strength)." And then he bit into the sausage to demonstrate what he had said. *Pikuach nefesh* — the saving of life — came before everything.

Papa watched as his father tried unsuccessfully to swallow the forbidden food. Then Grandfather turned and went out of the bunk and promptly threw up, spitting out the morsel his body was spiritually incapable of holding.

"He asked us to eat it even though he could not. He still taught me a lesson which lasted with me for the rest of my stay in these horrible places," my father told me.

I finish the blue background behind the embroidered tree, and look at my completed needlepoint. I see my son, Chaim, Hebrew for "life," and envision his marriage to Dahlia, my new daughter. A new life beginning with a fresh tree blossom. The tree branch growing upwards to *shamayim*, now branching again, beginning the next generation. Carrying on my grandfather's memory. Continuing the once weakened race. We are the lone branches, who had a chance to live so that the family line of Torah observing Jews would never die.

21. *Crowning of a Son*

I started to plant dahlias in our garden as soon as my son announced his engagement to Dahlia. I received some seeds from Yolanda, our housekeeper of thirty years, who was as excited as I was with the news of the upcoming wedding. I read the instructions on the back of the little paper packets. They would need lots of sun. I picked a spot for planting near the avocado tree and close to the hydrangea bushes, which carried their gorgeous blooms later on in the summer time. I planted the first seeds and handed the rest of them to Efram, our loyal gardener, to continue the job. Every *Shabbat* after lunch, I would go to my favorite piece of earth and watch as the first green sprouts appeared. At first I thought it was only my imagination when I saw something nobody else did.

"Look at the first dahlias," I said to my son.

"I don't see anything. Mami, you are dreaming."

Amazingly, the flowers did pop their heads out of the ground and everybody had to come and admire them. Even my elderly father-in-law

My 3 sons, oldest Tzvika (middle) the groom Chaimi and Erez with white rose in lapel.

wanted to see them and bent down slowly, trying to smell them. I watched my son, the groom, touch the delicate petals of a pink dahlia.

On June ninth, the wedding day, I got ready for the big event. My hair was coiffed and my makeup applied perfectly. I wore a dark red fitted gown and sling-back shoes.

I sat down on the terrace of our home and looked around. Waiters were busy loading the tables with food. We had a Hungarian food station with tiny stuffed cabbage in sweet tomato sauce, Schlishkele, and little oval matza balls rolled in a mixture of sugar and bread crumbs. A chef in a tall hat sharpened his shiny knives to carve smoked turkey, pastrami and corned beef.

A heat lamp brought out the pink color of the meat and kept it warm. Hundreds of sushi rolls — California, tuna, salmon, avocado and cucumber — were layered on silver plates around the water fountain in the front of the house. Large flower arrangements decorated each buffet table.

The *chuppa*, the little canopy under which the groom and bride were to be married, was built at the end of the garden, just before the tennis court steps. We commissioned an artist by the name of Shoshana to create a family heirloom in burgundy velvet fabric with cream-colored silk appliqués with writing in gold. Four wooden posts rested in earthen pots carrying the velvet roof. Dark red roses spilled out from the pots onto the ground. Four large arrangements crowned the four top corners of the *chuppa*, which was elevated on a platform covered with the Persian rug from our entry hall.

I knew that in less than an hour my father would stand under that *chuppa* welcoming the bride and groom, his grandchildren, the same way he had praised the liberators with his voice at the threshold of death in the concentration camp at Vaihingen-Enz. But this time he gave thanks to G-d for letting him survive until now to celebrate his grandchild's wedding day. There have been moments in my life when I felt particularly close to G-d, like at the birth of my sons; I knew this was going to be another great

My husband Raphy and I leading our son Chaimi to
the chuppa in our garden, 2002.

moment, when my father would sing and I would hold my son's hand to lead him to the steps to welcome his bride.

Six hundred white wooden chairs were set up on the tennis court for the invited guests to watch the ceremony. Three hundred chairs on each side of the court, divided by a red runner where the marching of the bride and groom would take place.

Two musicians played the clarinet and the flute near the throne where the bride would sit to receive her guests. The throne was a heavily gilded chair which I rented from a movie prop warehouse.

My three sons sat around a cocktail table entertaining each other. They were dressed in brand new black tuxedos and white pleated shirts. They all wore silvery ties in the same shade of blue. I watched them and my heart filled with pride. The older and younger son tried to keep the middle one calm. I think they told him jokes. They laughed together and the younger one patted his big brother's shoulder in a reassuring gesture.

I sucked it all in from the air: the sensation and the beauty surrounding me. I had achieved the highest point in my career as a mother — the crowning of a son.

And then it was all a blur. I took a deep breath and held on to my Dahlia's tiny soft hand to lead her to the throne and then I

Chaimi and Dahlia. Dahlia wearing my mother's
tiara, 2002.

smiled. I smiled for the next seven hours. I smiled at the Creator, who helped me find the right husband and give life to my son. I smiled at the One who let my son find his flower, his Dahlia, and I smiled at G-d who let the sun shine on that glorious day.

22. *Tante Piri*

Tante Piri opened the double doors of an old French armoire. Her arm disappeared behind a stack of linen.

"I can't reach it. You try," she said.

"What am I searching for?" I asked.

"A tin box, small like a shoe box."

"I got it."

Slowly Tante Piri carried her tired body towards the dining room table and sat with the old, yellowed container in her hands.

"Sit next to me, Pimpi," — that was my nickname — "You were always interested in family history and I feel very tired; maybe this is the last time I will see you."

I helped Tante Piri loosen the tight-shut lid of the old tea box. As she fingered each picture, her face was filled with memories. Each photograph symbolized an era long gone.

"This is my grandmother on my father's side."

I stared at the woman's serious face in the picture, and then wondered about the late nineteenth-century fashion. Sometimes Tante Piri

Tante Piri, sister of my mother's father, 1960.

concentrated for a few minutes as if she was going back in time, and then assertively, she would attach a name of a relative to the image in the photo. Her memory was impeccable. She was ninety-three years old when we went through that tin box. Yet her face was still almost wrinkle-free, and her blue eyes sparkled when she looked at me. She smiled when she gave me the old silver spice box tucked in among the photos as a gift.

In some ways Tante Piri was right when she said that this would be the last time I would see her. Though she was alive when I saw her a year later, her beautiful eyes were closed. Her strong heart was beating, but she had suffered a stroke and did not recognize me when I visited Budapest that fall of 1998.

"Look, Anyu (mother), can you believe who came to visit you, it's Pimpi all the way from Los Angeles." Andrea, her granddaughter, sat on one side of her bed and reluctantly gave up one of her grandmother's hands to me. The warmth of her body radiated from her hand into my heart.

Ivan, Tante Piri's son, lifted one of her eyelids to make her see me. She wore a beautiful, light pink, embroidered silk nightgown.

"Where is Tante Piri's old bed?"

"It's in storage till she feels better; this hospital bed is more practical for her right now."

I looked at the steel and metal contraption which my aunt rested on and thought about the beautiful brown oak bed she used to sleep on before she became sick. It was not only the bed I did not recognize — the entire room had been turned into a hospital room. In one corner stood something that functioned as a portable crane and an oxygen bottle was attached to the wall behind the bed. All the antique furniture had been removed, including the armoire where Tante Piri hid her photographs. The oil portrait of her as a young girl no longer hung on the wall near the window. What hit me the strongest was the smell of chemicals that filled the room instead of the light lavender aroma I was so familiar with. Three nurses were attending to her needs, pulling and prodding on all kinds of devices that kept her alive.

I could not imagine that this was the same room I slept in when I visited Budapest as a young girl.

Tante Piri, my mother's father's sister, was always so kind to me. Many times we went as a family to visit her, as we traveled to Budapest three or four times a year. But one time vividly remained in my mind. We were spending the Sukkot holidays in Budapest. My mother preferred to stay at the Hotel Royal in the city, close to the kosher restaurant, which was called "Nissel Vendeglö." Even before I knew I would marry into the Nissel family, we liked the food there. During *chol hamoed*, the intermediary days of the week-long holiday, I once was invited by my great-aunt to stay with her overnight in her large home on Rezoter 3. My ninth birthday was approaching and I felt all grown up and special to have the privilege to stay with her. After my family left to return to the hotel I started to unpack my small bag. It was really my mother's but for a few hours the bag was all mine. Tante Piri had beautiful blue eyes; I thought that they danced when she smiled at me.

"That's a beautiful dress you are unpacking. Is it new?" she asked me.

Mamuschka, my great-grandmother, mother of
Tante Piri.

"Yes, I just received it before Rosh Hashana. Mutti always buys us new clothes before the New Year."

This dress was special because it had so many gold buttons in front which, I thought, made the dress more valuable because of all that precious metal.

"I see one of the buttons is kind of loose. Tomorrow morning when there is better light outside I will sew it on for you."

Many times I thought that Tante Piri knew how to read my mind. I didn't have to tell her that I was afraid to lose one of these special buttons; she just knew.

We slept in her large carved oak bed, big enough for the two of us, Tante Piri in her customary silk nightgown. I felt like royalty sleeping there.

When the light was switched off, I listened to her telling me how her only son Ivan, who later became Hungary's most famous songwriter and playwright, survived the war.

"He ran most of the time, to escape the Nazis. And at the end of the war, when the Russians were approaching, there were no more vehicles available for transportation, so he walked for days from Vienna to Budapest."

I could not imagine a person walking so far. It took us more than four hours on the train to get to Budapest from Vienna.

Tante Piri always had interesting stories for

us. She would also tell me about the poet Chana Szenes, who was a niece of hers by marriage. Chana was from Budapest. During the war she escaped to Palestine, and she came back to Europe to try to save Jews. She parachuted into Hungary, was caught by the Nazis, and died for her heroism. She is a legend in Israel.

A sliver of moonlight shone through the delicate lace curtains reflecting on the gold buttons of my dress which Tante Piri had prepared on the outside of her armoire.

In the morning I woke up to the smell of fresh cocoa.

We appreciated these trips to Budapest so much because after the war, until 1961 nobody received a visa to cross the border into Communist Hungary. When we went for the first time, my great-grandmother, Tante Piri's mother, was still alive. Unfortunately she was confined to her bed and it was Tante Piri who tended to her at all times. We children entertained her with song and dance and poetry which Mamuschka would complete for us, remembering each one from her childhood.

"Children," she would say to us, "I went through two big wars."

Two wars was unimaginable to us; we thought that to survive one war was already incredible, and here we knew somebody who had gone through two.

We sat at the edge of her bed and she would

tell us how she survived. They hid in so-called safe houses established by diplomats like the famous Raoul Wallenberg. When it became dangerous to stay there, young Jewish people would come to warn them and then they had to move quickly to other hiding places.

Now Tante Piri looked even more frail than her mother had, all those years ago. Her eyes were closed, but I thought that maybe she heard me and so I started to talk to her as if we were still in her big oak bed having a lovely overnight together.

"Tante Piri, I am here, I came to visit you and tell you how my children are doing. Tzvika attends the university in Cambridge and is going to be a lawyer. Chaimi finished his economics degree and now works in his father's real estate office. Erez attends Jewish high school and is in tenth grade; he might have inherited his love for writing from you, Tante Piri."

I did not get any response. Gone was the Tante Piri who would recite poetry, give me clever advice for the future, or crack jokes to make me laugh. I loved her sense of humor very much. But, now, when I stroked her arm I felt her tiredness and realized how much things had changed since that time we revisited our ancestors in that tin box. I felt she needed her rest now. I bent down to touch her cheek and kissed her good-bye.

Now a picture of Tante Piri lies in the precious box she gave me. In October of 1999, at the age of ninety-six, she joined the faces she remembered so well. She went to laugh with them and show them the sparkle in her eyes.

23. *The Heidens*

A formal wedding picture is prominently displayed on the mantel of our fireplace in the living room. It was taken in 1925 when my grandmother's sister Dora Heiden married Rabbi Alexander Rosenberg of Yonkers, New York in Budapest. This photo always fascinated me, from the time I was a child.

"The police closed off the streets near the Kazinczy Shul to let the family's carriages come through," Mami would tell us.

We had just watched Princess Margaret, Queen Elizabeth's sister, exchange wedding vows. My sister and I crowded around a television set in the coffee shop around the corner from our home on Karlsplatz. Tante Dora's wedding picture now made perfect sense to us. Of course they'd had to close off the streets for my mother's family — they were royalty.

In the middle of the picture sat my Tante Dora, dressed in a lace gown, surrounded by her large family. A long veil was arranged around the leg of a square antique table, showing off its border in contrast with the dark

Persian carpets decorating the wedding hall. The elegant bride wore a white see-through hat trimmed with tiny flowers, which looked as though it had been forced onto her head; it was the latest fashion trend. She had good reason to smile — she had just married the handsome dark-haired and bearded young man standing at her side. He stood out taller and wider than anybody in the family, an imposing figure surrounded by his new aristocratic family.

We were lucky enough to know this dignified man, our great uncle Alex, who visited us twice a year when he was in Europe on business.

"Uncle Alex is coming, Uncle Alex is coming!" my father would announce and everybody would scramble to get ready for the important visitor who would fly in the same day or the next to crown our *Shabbat* table with his presence.

My mother was the busiest. She cooked up a storm: stuffed veal, chicken, Lokschenkigel (a noodle dish) and potato kugel. My father prepared the carp, his specialty, and ground the horseradish to garnish the fish. My sister Mona would shout out her instructions to me and my little brother Tomi to clean up our stuff. All our clothes, heaped on different chairs, were quickly hung in the closet. Books stacked on tables would be filed on their proper bookshelves, a white starched tablecloth, gleaming silverware and the special Cobalt china placed on the dining room table, and Mami would light the *Shabbat* candles. Then we waited, my mother, sister and I, for the men to come home from *shul*. Once Uncle Alex entered, the entire room lit up with his presence. His dark eyes gleamed when he smiled at us, and we were happy.

My father gladly gave up his seat at the head of the table for this distinguished relative. "Would Uncle Alex please take his seat right here?" Papa would gently pull out the green velvet upholstered chair to make it easier for Uncle Alex to sit down as we stood around the table waiting for our visitor to take his place.

My parents taught us that important people need to be addressed in the third person. "Would Uncle Alex like red or white wine?" my father would ask, or, "Would Uncle Alex like to sing *zemirot* now?"

When the singing began, Uncle Alex would hit his fist on the table in rhythm with the songs and many of the forks and knives jumped from their neatly arranged spots next to the plates in harmony with our singing.

Once the food was served, we knew why he loved to come and spend *Shabbat* with us. Well, yes, he loved our family, that's for sure, but he also indulged in Mami's food. Uncle Alex's plate was heaped up high with the meats and kugels. "Too much, Ildiko," he would protest every time Mami placed another plate of food in front of him, but in the end he ate it all.

When we walked to the park on *Shabbat* afternoons and Uncle Alex held my hand, I watched how everybody on the street would turn around to stare at him with admiration. He was extremely handsome and always wore a black suit, white shirt and black bow tie. His black hat matched the black raincoat he either wore or carried on his arm. But it wasn't only his clothes; Uncle Alex had a noble appearance, with his impressive height, neatly trimmed white beard, long fingers and dancing eyes. He was a commanding presence even in his later years. His long fingers would wrap around my small hands and I held on to them tightly. Uncle Alex made me feel comforted, warm and proud, all at the same time. Sometimes when he would smile at me I knew he would begin telling one of his amazing stories.

Uncle Alex was the closest thing we had to a grandfather and we were the happiest kids on earth when he came to visit our home. The walls of the house were shouting, "Uncle Alex! Uncle Alex!" long after he left.

We stared at the wedding photo, awed by the sight of our beloved great uncle as a young man; his eyes still glowed the way they did in the pictures.

"Who are all these other people in the picture, Mami?" I would ask, never tiring of the

Uncle Alex's wedding picture, 1927.

descriptions my mother would give of each
member of her late family.

"All the way on the left behind my mother,
that's Uncle Sanyi, you remember him? He
came with Tante Eva to visit us last year when
we were still in the old apartment."

Uncle Sanyi survived the war in Algiers and
settled in Antwerp, Belgium after the war. In the
picture with his family he had the appearance of
maybe a sixteen-year-old lad who had just
started to realize what life was all about. He
stared at the camera with a curious but stern
look, more or less like all of the family members
in the picture. Maybe at the time it was not
proper to smile for a photograph, or maybe the
reason for their seriousness was the fact that my

Tante Dora was leaving her family in Budapest behind. She was about to cross the great Atlantic Ocean to move with her husband to New York.

We knew Uncle Sanyi from the trips he took to come visit us. He would entertain us children with jokes; once he demonstrated his sense of humor by cutting a piece of orange peel in the shape of gorilla teeth. He slid the peel under his lips and hopped around the table making us laugh with the scary orange piece in his mouth.

A visit to Muhlhauser, the largest toy store in Vienna, was a special treat we looked forward to every time Uncle Sanyi came to town.

"Take whatever your heart desires!" he would announce.

Mona and I stared at the famous Barbie dolls freshly imported from America.

"Mami said we should pick something reasonable," Mona told me. Slowly we turned from our favorite spot in the store and wandered towards the stacked up family games. We knew Uncle Sanyi really meant what he said, but we honored our mother's instructions. We chose a set which contained six different board games in one box — enough to last a lifetime in our youth. Every rainy afternoon or after lunch we reached for the gift Uncle Sanyi had let us choose that day in Muhlhauser. We used those games till the black and white color of the pawns wore off and could only be differentiated by tiny specks of color.

It was not the presents he bought us that brought us the joy, although of course we did enjoy his gifts, but it was the fact that Uncle Sanyi represented the royalty which Mami talked about when we stared at the faces of the Heiden family in that old wedding photo. Even the sense of being surrounded by all these toys in the store was enough to make us feel glorious. He represented glitz, glamour and elegance, all the finery of Mami's youth: leather suitcases, fine hotels, silk pajamas, black pearls, satin and crocodile shoes, large dining room tables and servants around the clock. And most of all, my mother's ancestors of whom she was so proud. Uncle Sanyi was the one who continued the family business working with precious jewels, establishing a name which was known for honesty and integrity.

But in the end the most important venture Uncle Sanyi took upon himself was his dedication to and love for Jerusalem. He bought an apartment in the newly built Plaza Hotel in the capital of Israel and there he spent all the Jewish holidays where his spirits found new heights. He was even recognized by Mayor Ehud Olmert, who made Uncle Sanyi an honorary citizen of Jerusalem for his contribution to the city. We, his grand-nieces and nephews, learned a lot from this man who wanted to engulf his family with his smile and graciousness. We will forever remember him.

Mami's stories and the strong presence of our Uncle Alex and our Uncle Sanyi and Tante Eva made the Heiden family come alive for us instead of remaining figures in a dusty old photo. Even though so many of the family were gone, and their prewar way of life disappeared forever, we felt the "nobility" of the Heiden family and shared Mami's pride in her family history.

24. *Road Trip to Romania*

Shlomo, our driver, had no idea how to get to Rudolf Utca Street, so he asked a local cab driver for directions.

"Give me twenty Lei and I will lead you there," said the cab driver.

We had a hard time seeing the gray car in front of us with all the exhaust fumes it gave off in front of the windshield. But we were used to the fact that Romanian cars pollute the air considerably.

We arrived at Rudolf Utca 10. The street looked like any other road in Eastern Europe. The only difference was that this was the street where my father spent his childhood years until he was sent to a small town called Krasna to attend yeshiva. This was also the street from where our entire family was deported, first to the Jewish ghetto and then to Auschwitz-Birkenau. It was almost impossible to imagine the SS troops storming into the buildings and rounding up the Jews — it was such a calm and quiet street.

Trees lined the cobblestone sidewalks and

gates protected most of the homes from any form of violence.

I knocked at the door of a one-story stucco home. A small boy opened the door and told me that his mother was sleeping.

"Could you please wake up your mother? I came all the way from America to talk to her."

The boy disappeared behind the wooden door and I was left standing in the courtyard for quite a while. At one time this house was filled with Jews; not just any Jews, but my father's family. My family. As I stood waiting I imagined what happened during Passover in that court-yard: "Malki, Peru, come help me carry the carpets back into the house," my grandmother would call to her two daughters as she cleaned for Passover. My aunts brought their own children along for the cleaning. I could hear my grandfather singing, old ancient tunes handed down from one generation to the next.

If I listened carefully I could even hear the youngest grandchild singing the "*Ma Nishtana*," otherwise known as the Four Questions of the Seder night. But now, it was a rundown build-ing, a skeleton of what once was. The soul of it was extinguished in 1944 and all that was left were the memories of happy times.

"Open the door, Nussi, Eliahu Hanavi would like to enter!" my grandfather would tell my father at the point in the Seder when the door is opened for Elijah the Prophet. Which door did my father open? Was it the one I stood in front of at this moment or was it the wood framed door in the corner of the building?

"Hello, can I help you?" A lady stepped out from the apartment that I had knocked on previously.

"This is the house where my father lived before the war. Do you remember the Liebermann family?"

"I've only lived here for a few years but Mrs. Klein has been here for many years, maybe she remembers your family." She walked over to her neighbor's apartment and knocked at the door.

"Mrs. Klein, there is somebody here from America. Open the door," she said.

Slowly the door opened a tiny bit and all I saw were strands of hair flooding around her face, some of them coiled around her ears but most having lost their pins. It was gray, wiry hair, grown out of control with age. Tired eyes blinked at me through the hair with suspicion.

"Come out, this lady wants to ask you something," the neighbor coaxed her, trying to make her leave the darkness of her own four walls.

Slowly Mrs. Klein stepped out into the gray, wet day. A short-necked, humped-over figure approached me cautiously. I wondered if she had lived here before the war, if she was capable of remembering anything. She seemed to be part of the past; as if history was written in each wrinkle. She wore an old worn wool jacket, the kind my father wore at home when he was cold, but hers had moth holes in it. The only thing colorful was the apron she wore around her large body.

"Do you remember the Liebermann family who lived here sixty years ago?" I asked her.

At this moment a smile emerged from somewhere deep inside her and I imagined her face unburdened from all the years she carried. Youth returned to her when she said: "Toby Neni, Hershy Baci, yes, I remember. They lived here, right here."

I got so excited with her outburst of memories, I wanted to hug her.

"I am their granddaughter and these are their great-grandchildren." And I pointed to my three sons who gathered around me.

She smiled and cried at the same time and repeated my grandparents' names in Hungarian over and over again.

"What do you remember about them?" I asked.

"They are all gone. The Nazis took them and I am the only one left here," she said.

After a while I realized that even though she remembered my grandparents she could not tell me anything other than the fact that my family's bakery still existed only a few blocks down the road. She also told me that she was married to a Jew but he died a few years ago and that's when her face lost its glow. With that she slipped back into the present and the burden of her years returned to her face.

I had the feeling that we were tiring her and I stepped backwards motioning to my family that it would be better if we would leave now.

She blessed me Hungarian style and we hugged good-bye. When I looked back as we climbed into our van I realized she was still standing in the same place. I stared at the rear-view mirror and watched my grandparents' home disappear in the horizon.

After a five-minute drive, we found the bakery that belonged to my family. We walked through the green front door with dirty glass panels. Shelves of bread were lined up on a wall behind the counter. It looked like nothing had changed since before the war. A customer asked for half a loaf of bread and the lady behind the counter took a large knife whose wooden handle was so worn that the blade looked as if it would cut through her hand.

Was this the same knife my father used when he was helping out at the bakery?

In front of the counter the customer had placed her dirty wet wicker shopping basket on a narrow shelf I thought would collapse with a small gust of wind. The wooden shelves held dark, round, firm bread sprinkled with white dots of flour, displayed like Wedgewood plates in an old English manor house. The delicious scent of bread lingered in the air and warmed my nostrils.

The customer grabbed her wet basket and left the store, dripping as she walked past me.

"*Jonapot kivanok*," I greeted in Hungarian.

"Which bread would you like and do you want the entire wheel or just half of it?" she asked me.

"This bakery belonged to my family before the war," I said. "Do you know anything about it?"

But to the young salesgirls my question didn't mean much.

"Really, I knew it was old, this place, but I did not know that old," she stated and then again asked if I wanted any bread.

We left through the green entrance door with a round wheel of bread wrapped in newspaper under my arm. I held onto the bread tightly; almost immediately its smell permeated the air of our van.

The last stop I wanted to make in Cluj was the Jewish cemetery. Shlomo, our driver, dropped my family off at our hotel and I continued for about a half-hour drive to the gates of the cemetery. I opened the squeaky old gates and knocked at the door of an old shack.

A non-Jewish couple were the caretakers of these holy grounds.

"I am looking for Hellman, my father's

mother's father... could you please tell me where I could find his grave?" I asked.

"Do you want to visit only his grave or other family members too?" he asked me.

I did not know exactly whom he was talking about but I said yes anyway. He reached for a very large, worn book from inside a drawer of a table and started turning the pages carefully till he ended up on the page with the letter *H*.

How he could decipher anything in this ancient book was a mystery to me but I guess he was an expert. After a few minutes of searching he took a piece of paper and jotted numbers and letters. "Come, I will show you around," he said.

We walked through the old cemetery, passing tilted and broken gravestones. It was filled with stones that were no longer legible. Not even the names or dates of buried Jews could be deciphered.

I arrived at the grave of a great-uncle who had passed away before the war. I took my *Tehillim* from my pocketbook and recited some Psalms in his memory.

"Tell the sons and daughter who live in Israel that they have to fix this grave. It all sunk into the earth. That happens a lot after so many years," the caretaker said. I promised to tell my father's relatives to take care of it and then continued to visit different graves of family members who had died of old age or illness before the war. They were the lucky ones; the relatives who died during the war weren't granted the privilege of a funeral and a gravestone, much less dying of old age.

It was time to say the afternoon prayer and I faced what I believed was east towards Jerusalem. I saw myself as one of the last of the Mohicans. Who will ever come again here to this forgotten piece of holy land to visit ancient graves? I was unwilling to leave but my feet carried me in the direction of the gate. I headed back to the honking cars and the modernity of the outside world.

25. Yesh Lev (There Is a Heart)

I received a phone call from Rivka, my patient's mother, last week on Tuesday afternoon.

"*Yesh lev!* (There is a heart!)"

My car swerved to the right and then to the left. I made a U-turn in the middle of the road and headed towards UCLA Medical Center. My car seemed to fly as my heartbeat raced down Sunset Boulevard. I wanted to be there before the team wheeled Mordechai into surgery.

Twenty-eight-year-old Mordechai arrived from Israel for a heart transplant just four months ago. He was born with only one ventricle instead of two and had to undergo numerous procedures and four heart surgeries in Israel in order to survive until now. I met him for the first time a few days after he arrived in Los Angeles with his mother Rivka and younger brother Aviel. I could not believe that he was already twenty-eight years old. He looked sixteen, maybe seventeen, but not more. Though crossing the world to find a heart is not an impossible task nowadays, Mordechai's journey to find a heart touched my own.

I meet these families through an organization called Bikur Cholim (visiting the sick). A group of volunteers from all over Los Angeles receive a fax once a week with the names of patients in different hospitals. They are sick people who, for various reasons, don't receive visitors. They are either from out of state, or they don't have family and friends here in Los Angeles. Usually I receive a personal phone call from Rabbi Ten, the director of Bikur Cholim, if he is expecting an Israeli family, because of my ability to speak a little bit of Hebrew. I serve as a mediator between the medical team and the patient.

By now, I am so familiar with most of the hospitals in the city that I enter as if I were one of the doctors or nurses, with one little difference: I have no higher degree. My "degree" comes directly from above, from G-d Himself, who placed me on earth to try to help heal with kind words. Sometimes I receive phone calls from all over the world from strangers who want me to match them up with doctors I have befriended over the years.

"You are just like my mother was," my father told me the other day.

My grandmother, may she rest in peace, helped the sick in Romania before the war, establishing good relationships with the local doctors.

I could not wait to get to UCLA Hospital in

Westwood and see the happy face of my new friend and his family. Even though I had only known him for a few weeks, I felt like he was a close relative for whom I cared deeply. Every patient I meet is different. But maybe because Mordechai was so young and so eager to live, I was automatically pulled into his quest for life. I was very impressed with the knowledge he possessed of his condition. He knew how to disconnect and reconnect his IV, and he read the results of his echogram or cardiogram. He was like a doctor himself or at least like a nurse. I appreciated the fact that they were so optimistic and full of hope: he, the patient who had to endure so much pain but never gave up, and his family, who supported him.

I heard Rivka's voice from the hallway. She was speaking to somebody on the phone in Hebrew.

"*Yesh lev!* (There is a heart!)"

The phone kept ringing for most of the hour of my visit. Always the same two words, "*Yesh lev!*"

Rivka did not even say hello or good-bye. Nothing else counted, only these two words, which meant so much.

Mordechai raised his skinny, yellowish arms up high.

"I am going to have a healthy heart, I am going to have another chance at life!" he shouted. His brown eyes told a story of hope. In his excitement he uncovered his frail body. I could not avoid the sight in front of me. What I saw was an enlarged belly the size of a balloon, punctuated by a scar that made its way up almost the entire length of his torso, not a straight road, more like a trail in a forest with all of the signs placed on a hazardous road. A large gauze pad, attached with Band-Aids, covered different wounds on his hip where his surgeons had performed biopsies a few days before.

Rivka finally got off the phone. She started to explain to me more about the scars on her son's body.

"This is from the first procedure, and that one from the second surgery. And here he had a terrible rash yesterday, the doctors could not diagnose it," she said.

It was like looking at a road map, trying to find your way to your final destination. Rivka called it history.

One of the transplant nurses walked into the room.

"Are you ready, Mordechai?" she asked. "Dr. Laks looked at the heart and he said that this one is perfect for you. He said you needed a heart that was neither really small nor large, a middle-sized heart, like that of an eighteen- or nineteen-year-old teenager," she said.

I imagined Dr. Laks standing in a well-lit room with Mordechai's heart in an icebox. Perhaps he took it out while wearing surgical gloves, carefully weighing it on a baby scale, touching it and then identifying the ventricles, to see if both were there. Maybe he wanted to feel it in his hands, like a rehearsal before the real surgery. In my mind I could hear him say, "It will be good for Mordechai."

The nurse left the room and wished him a speedy recovery. I left the room too. I walked past the large rooftop window where just the day before Rivka and I had watched a helicopter land.

"Maybe they've brought a heart for my son?" she had wondered.

Mordechai was wheeled into the surgery room a couple of hours after I left the hospital.

I hurried home to call my oldest son, Tzvika, whose birthday was that same day. How strange it was to realize that both young men were twenty-eight years old, and both mothers carried the name Rivka. But that's where the coincidences ended.

I remember when I gave birth to my son on March 4, 1975, when I was twenty-one years old; an almost ten-pound beautiful baby boy. The nurses and the doctor passed him around like a chef would to an audience after he had completed the perfect chocolate soufflé.

"Now, that's what we call a perfect, healthy baby," they said.

Only many years later, when I stood in front of Mordechai's bed in the ICU of the UCLA

Medical Center, did I understand the true meaning of that statement.

Mordechai's mother, the other Rivka, also gave birth around the same time as I. But she had known from the start what it was like to be at her son's side, to ease his pain, dry his tears, find the right doctors, and travel all the way to California to give birth again.

She stood in the ICU and smiled at me, even though her son looked more dead than alive after the fifteen-hour heart transplant surgery.

Two nurses attended to Mordechai. I watched the male nurse, Lee, turning knobs on what seemed to me like twenty different machines attached to the patient. Lee drained fluid from one plastic hose and filled a little bottle or ziplock bag with another liquid. Then he stored them, sealed them and wrote on them with a black marker. A female nurse named Claudia was engrossed in a computer in front of the bed. She read things from ten different screens and then frantically entered data into the computer. On the right side of the bed, I saw a large machine, which pumped blood through plastic transparent hoses. I heard beeping noises and wondered how the attending nurses identified which beep belonged to which machine and how they knew that they had to turn the knob to the right and not to the left on one or the other machine.

Mordechai's eyes were covered with white

five-inch square gauze patches, perhaps so that the bright lights would not disturb his artificially induced sleep. I was glad he was asleep and did not see me, because I was in shock. The surgeon had left open a hole, an approximately five-inch hole in his chest cavity that displayed Mordechai's heart. It was only covered with a see-through plastic wrap, like the type I use in my kitchen.

Rivka stood next to me and explained that they had to leave that opening for the sake of observation over the next couple of days. I always thought that looking at beautiful blooming wisteria trees in the springtime proved to me who the Creator was. But at that instant, staring at a real heart pumping life into a twenty-eight-year-old young man, I could really feel G-d's presence.

An entire shift of young interns came to look at the patient. As I walked away from the ICU, I heard the voice of the white-coated young doctor explaining the complexities of the surgery.

Rivka walked out with me. We took the elevator to the ground floor and emerged into the sun.

"I need some fresh air," she said.

The sky was a deep blue and the red bougainvillea curled around a light pole just in front of the gray walls of the hospital. Springtime is like the rebirth of nature. I always wondered about the mystique of everything that bloomed, the wonders of a love relationship between nature and G-d. But on that day, I saw the love relationship between a human being and G-d, with the surgeon performing the angelic task of saving a life.

I imagined the doctor standing in front of the patient's bed in the recovery room. He stood there uttering a silent prayer: "I did what I was taught to do. Now it is in Your hands."

The feelings of survival I felt leaving the hospital that day reminded me of my fragile father who willed to live against all odds, and won.

26. The Libeskind Museum

A navy blue uniformed museum guide pushed the heavy silver metal door open. I am alone in the remembrance tower of the Libeskind Museum in Berlin. I came to visit my niece Joelle — the same one who married in Zurich the day after my family visited Kaufering. She now lives in Berlin with her husband and my parents' first great-granddaughter. I am here for a family visit, yet wherever I go I always am compelled to enter the Jewish museums. It is almost completely dark outside, twilight time. I look up and stare at the tall, dark, never-ending towers. Small light beams from the outside shine through the oddly shaped windows in the building. I hear noises from the street, the faint rumbling of the tram, cars squeaking to a halt and distant dogs barking. It all sounds like it is coming from far away.

I browse through the interior part of the museum; it doesn't capture my attention. My mind is somewhere else. I am outside now. I find myself in The Garden of Exile and Emigration. Forty-nine concrete columns stand at an incline and I am trapped inside. The gravel under my feet crunches, reminding me of the famous shortcuts my husband has taken me through when we walk to the Kotel (Wailing Wall) in Jerusalem. I feel trapped. The unbelievable cold and darkness surrounds me.

Where should I go?

I make my legs lift my feet.

Crunch, crunch.

Suddenly I bump into a sharp corner, my nose stuck between two walls that come together at a point. Dead end!

Every direction leads me to another dead end. It seems like there is no way out of this outside tower maze.

I am alone with my thoughts; horrible memories of my father's tales become so real. No underwear, no shoes. Completely drained of all of life's physical sustenance. I can see him behind the electrical barbed wire fences in Auschwitz-Birkenau. How can someone in a thin cotton pajama stand for a twenty-hour roll call in the cold dark?

With one broken eyeglass he tried to imagine life outside the fences. He faintly heard a tractor rumble as it mowed the nearby fields. "Hello, is anybody out there? How come no one can hear me cry?" Nobody saw the whips in the hands of the uniformed soldiers who beat the children, and nobody smelled the human smoke rising from the crematorium tower. It was as if the barbed wire around the camps wound tightly around the Germans' and Poles' hearts.

It is cold in Berlin, thirteen below zero Celsius. I am not wearing gloves. Most of my outerwear is checked in the coatroom of the museum. I lean my body against the cold black granite. I want to feel what my father felt throughout these months of bitter cold. Instead the sensation of what it means to be cold seems to drain out of me. I hear my father say, "I was numb, frozen with pain standing there for hours. I stopped feeling it at all."

Suddenly from somewhere in the building a small voice travels, "Momma, Momma!"

It is my little niece and namesake, Rebecca. I follow her voice and retrace my steps through the maze. I open the heavy doors with my icy bare hands and see a smile beaming from the face of this one-year-old little girl. Suddenly, as the doors slam shut behind me, I realize that out of the dark, cold, horror of burning towers, a light breaks through and opens the doors for generations to come.

But now, as I slowly walk home, I shiver. Even though I am wearing wool stockings, a cashmere sweater, a pashmina shawl, my dark brown winter coat and boots, the cold chills my bones. I pull my cap tightly over my ears and eyes to cover my frozen tears. Berlin — the city where all the orders came from to destroy a race, to butcher an entire people — this was the High Command Center. It all started here.

My niece had been reluctant to settle here in this place, but her husband, Rabbi Josh Spinner, is working with the Lauder Foundation to reestablish *Yiddishkeit* — Judaism — in this place that Hitler tried to make *Judenrein*, empty of Jews. He is bringing back lost souls, returning them to the traditions of their ancestors, repairing the ruptures. Just as so many died here *al kiddush Hashem*, for a sanctification of G-d's name, my niece and her husband live here *al kiddush Hashem*. Living in Berlin is not a choice they made for their own benefit; it is a duty they know they must fulfill for the sole purpose of saving young immigrant Jews who have lost their heritage. They are indeed the light breaking through and opening the doors for generations to come.

27. *Der Kleine Eli*

I was walking with my sister Mona on 5th Avenue when I received an urgent phone call from my daughter-in-law Dahlia: "Eli made four steps!"

I almost dropped all my shopping bags.

"I can't believe it. Are you sure, all by himself? But he's not even eleven months old yet. My grandchild is a genius!" I responded with glee.

"What's going on?" Mona asked.

"Eli is walking! He made his first steps all by himself, on his own two legs." I wanted to announce it to the entire city of Manhattan. But I changed my mind as I thought of my father; he's always telling me that all Jewish grandchildren are geniuses and that I should not make a big fuss about Eli.

Eli was born on May 31 at about 2:30 in the afternoon. I had just landed at Los Angeles airport, LAX, returning from a trip to Israel for the holidays and Vienna to visit my parents. A few days before I was supposed to return to America I received a call from the soon-to-be father:

"Mami, maybe you should come home earlier. Dahlia's doctor said the baby could be a couple of weeks early."

That was it, that's all I needed to hear. I did not want to miss the arrival of my first grandchild. I packed my little carry-on bag and called a taxi driver in Vienna, Herr Sotola. I promised him a fat tip if he got me to the airport in time for a flight I didn't even have a seat for yet. He raced through a part of Vienna I did not recognize from my childhood, but I did not ask him too many questions so he could concentrate on weaving through the rush-hour traffic. He got me there just in time.

I arrived in Los Angeles via Zurich at 1:45

Our first grandchild, Eli, 2005.

P.M. As soon as we landed I switched on my cell phone and received a text message from my son. "ETA 2 P.M." Usually these words are reserved for planes, but my son referred to the arrival of his first baby. There was a long line at the passport aisles and I began to panic.

"Excuse me, could you let me through? I am expecting my first grandchild right now, at this moment." I said those words at least ten times before I stood first in line in front of the immigration officer.

"I am becoming a grandmother right now," I said to the solemn, uniformed man behind the counter. At first he pretended not to hear me, but then as I insisted that he acknowledge this important fact, he quickly congratulated me.

"What is the purpose of your trip?" he asked me.

"Who cares?" I thought, but then I realized that he was more interested in the status of my passport than in my becoming a grandmother.

"Family visit," I answered.

Thankfully he was satisfied with this explanation and smacked a loud stamp onto one of the pages in my passport.

Then I ran. I was so glad I had not checked in any luggage and hoped my son Tzvika would be outside waiting for me. He is a good driver and would get me to the hospital fast.

"What is it? What is it?" I asked my son the second I spotted him.

"Not here yet, Dahlia is in the delivery room," he answered.

When we finally arrived at the hospital I jumped into the elevator. Just as I was between the ground floor and plaza level my cell phone beeped again announcing a new text message. I had a grandson!

The rest is history. Once the little bundle of joy was gently placed into my arms I was smitten. I completely fell in love with what to my eyes is the smartest and most beautiful boy in the whole wide world. When he smiled at me just a few days after he came home from the hospital, I knew he recognized me already. And when he began to lift his head once inch off the mattress I knew it was to say hello to me.

Every one of his little actions was celebrated with hurrahs and bravos. Little Eli, or Der Kleine Eli, as I call him, would receive the self-confidence he needs in order to become a leader in the Jewish community. He represents one of the millions of grandchildren born into this world simply to be surrounded by the love of their parents and grandparents. Thankfully he is lucky enough to have two complete sets of grandparents and even a few great-grandparents.

I never knew what it meant to have grandparents. My generation was robbed of that because of the Holocaust. I had one grandmother who survived the Bergen-Belsen concentration camp and then immigrated to Israel. The rest I never knew. My mother's mother — Omama, as we called her — lived in Givat Ayin. We had to write her letters every Friday on Aerograms, a one-page light blue sheet of paper that didn't require any stamps. My mother licked the seal after I drew a nice vase with flowers and wrote, "Many kisses from Rebecca." That was my relationship with Omama. I only met her once when I was six years old and we went on a trip to Israel. I remember the strange feeling of not knowing what to expect from a grandparent. I didn't know how she was supposed to act. Unfortunately I never got to know her any better; that was the last time I met her, for she passed away when I was ten.

Why are there no books on how to raise grandbabies? There are hundreds of them on how to bring up the perfect son or daughter and yet none for grandparents! And so, I did what I always wanted to do with my own children but Dr. Spock would not allow. I spoiled him!

"Now that Eli can take steps on his own, we have to celebrate," I told Mona after we arrived home. I opened my finest bottle of champagne and celebrated my grandchild's first steps on his own two feet. I celebrated for my parents who now could see the next generation. We're still here.

28. *The Ruby Ring*

Whenever Mutti and Papa went out for the evening, and we were tired of listening to the radio,
we would go exploring. We opened up drawers
and cabinets looking to find something to dis-
tract our attention until bedtime. We never
touched the china that was cramped into one of
the credenzas behind the dining room table, but
the two large drawers in the wall cabinets were
permitted. That's where the good silver and
other luxurious items were kept. Mutti did not
mind us playing with these valuable items; in
fact many times, when she wanted to explain
the memories behind the precious items, she
would explore the drawers with us. She wanted
us to have the same passion she did for beautiful things, which she gathered over her lifetime.

At first we pulled out our favorite piece, the
coral red satin purse Mutti wore out on fancy
evenings. It had been loved so much and used
so often that the fabric was ripped at the edges,
and some of the tiny seed pears were hanging
on their last thread. But we didn't notice that it
was falling apart; all we could remember was

how magical Mutti looked before one of the elegant parties she and Papa attended. She would stand by the door in her red satin dress, bought at "Adlmuller," holding the purse with her long shiny evening gloves. We were not sure if Mutti had the purse first and then bought the dress to match, but the color was exactly the same, a dark coral red. How could we ever forget the way she looked? Her dark thick hair was carefully arranged in an up-do, following the style of Farah Diba, the recently crowned Empress of Iran. It was as popular as Jackie Kennedy's short bob, when she became the First Lady. We loved Mutti's silk heels, which matched the outfit in the same red. To add what she called a little "*Pfiff*," or a little fancy addition, she clipped her faux earrings onto the front of her shoes. It was amazing how she turned one item she owned into another one.

When we had removed the largest items from the drawer, Tomi, the youngest and the one with the smallest hands, was always selected to reach for the treasures hidden in the back of the drawer. Mutti told us that she had to call Derek, the handyman, to fix the drawer, but she was always too busy with our store and us children. Tomi reached behind the silver tea-spoons with quartz handles and pushed aside the silver cigarette boxes that my father had used in his smoking days.

"I think I have it," he said.

Slowly, with half of his body inside the drawer as we held him by his feet, he reached for the precious box. He was only six years old and was not tall enough to do it on his own. When we saw something green, we plopped Tomi on the floor and did the rest ourselves. The box was made of malachite, a semiprecious stone of all shades of green. The lid had geometrical carvings and we went over it with our fingers many times to feel the indentation. The stone was heavy and felt cold to the touch. It contained pieces of jewelry Mutti had received when she was a little girl and other items she had from her childhood in Budapest. Just as our mother had done when she was a girl, we played with the beautiful colored stones that formed my mother's childhood memories.

We opened the lid and tried on a small gold ring with two tiny pears strung on a thin wire. Tiny splinters of diamonds were placed in a triangle setting.

"I can't get it off," I said to Mona.

"I'll do it," Mona assured me, but she could not do it either.

I had once seen Mutti soaping her finger to take a ring off. We ran into the bathroom and I soaped my little finger, which was almost the color purple. It finally came off and we hastily returned the little ring to its rightful spot.

After rummaging around a bit more we found two loose green rectangle stones; Mutti taught us that these were called emeralds. Another few small light blue stones in oval shape were right next to the emeralds. Mutti called those aquamarines. They were the same color as Mona's eyes. We sat talking about how the stones reminded us of the pebbles on the beach of Opatiy, our summer vacation spot in Yugoslavia. Mutti bought us special white plastic shoes so that we could walk on the sand without hurting our feet.

As we opened the bottom compartment of the box we stared at the empty gold setting that sat alone between two plush cushions. It once was the famous ruby ring. The hole that held the ruby was very large, about the size of my thumbnail. It was Mutti's favorite ring; she talked to it and believed that it was her lucky charm.

Mutti had gone out with Papa one night and had forgotten the ring on the counter. I woke up to screaming: "Inge, please give me back my ring. I received this from my grandmother," my mother pleaded with our babysitter.

"It's my ring," we heard Inge say.

"No, I can prove to you it's mine," Mutti said with fervor in her voice, "Take it off; I'll show you it's mine!"

As I walked into the kitchen I saw my mother hold her ring up to the white plastic lamp hanging from the ceiling. "Come close and you will see the initial *H* engraved into the stone. It stands for Heiden, the name of my grandfather's store."

Every piece of jewelry my mother received from her family had this initial engraved on it. Inge couldn't get away with stealing it.

My parents did not file charges with the police, because they had known Inge's mother for a long time and felt that this was enough of a lesson and that she would never steal again. However, we always had different babysitters after that.

Mutti never took off that ring; it was so strange that she forgot it that night. She must have taken it off to do her housecleaning; rubies are a very soft stone and she probably didn't want to damage it.

"Rebecca," she would tell me, "this stone connects me to my grandparents. I am so afraid that if I lose it, my connection to them will be gone."

Mutti grew up in her grandparents' house with her mother. Her father had passed away when she was two. It's almost as if the ring provided her with a physical connection to her grandparents. She was petrified to lose the ring and with it those she loved so dearly.

We will never forget the day the ruby fell out of the setting; it was a day of mourning. I know it sounds ridiculous but that's how my mother felt. She was so attached to that ruby, which she had received from her grandmother who died shortly after the war. She saw it as her mystical and wondrous companion. We walked up and down Kartnerstrasse the entire day until it was too dark to look for the stone. Mutti claimed that's where she lost it, but we never found it. The gold setting lay in the box, like a skeleton from ancient times.

We closed the box and pushed it all the way back into the drawer.

It was ten o'clock, our bedtime, and we went to sleep. We talked in the dark about the times Mutti told us that she was raised like a princess in a big house with servants. We imagined her wearing that precious ruby ring around her finger and walking out the door with her matching ruby purse. She showed us how to see beauty in this world. She taught us that we shouldn't walk by without noticing the magnif-icence in life. As we played with those ancient things of a time long gone, we built our lives on memories.

Mutti's fear that the connection with her past would be severed if she didn't have the ruby anymore proved unfounded. The memo-ries remained even though those days were long gone, shattered by the Nazis and the pas-sage of time. There were so many irreplaceable lost precious jewels in our family. Ripped from their settings, their lives cruelly cut short, they left gaping, unfillable holes in our lives. And yet, the strong, enduring gold housing that had held them was still there for us. We still lived a Torah life in the way that our ancestors had before us. The structure was still intact, still valuable, still beautiful.

Now and then I still see those precious jewels shimmering, in the eyes of my children and grandchild. They may have been taken from us, but nothing could ever extinguish their sparkle.

29. *Floaters*

I build on the stories which were passed on to me by my father, mother and other family members. Without that foundation I would be standing on nothing but air. Just as a house without a sturdy foundation can start to collapse when a little earthquake strikes, the same is true for human beings whose foundations are shaky. Once a little problem hits them they fall into pieces.

Nobody told them stories to hold them up. They don't know how their great-grandfather survived the pogroms in Russia and their great-grandaunt gave birth to her youngest child in the middle of a forest with a friend assisting so that the Nazis would not find them. I think of people who try to establish their lives without the foundation of these family stories as "floaters."

They never had a great-aunt like my Tante Piri who elaborated on the escape of her son who marched on foot from Vienna to Budapest. Floaters never listened to a great-grandmother reciting children's poems at age 86, never sat on their grandfather's lap to listen to his wise words and learn of their family lore.

Those who did not attend Jewish schools often fell prey to the hatred of the non-Jew. Without a solid knowledge of their own traditions, all they knew was what the non-Jews reflected back to them: Jews had hook noses and killed their G-d.

At the end of their school day, floaters would leave their prayer book — if they even ever had one — at home in a dusty corner, hidden from their fearful eyes. Floaters were quick to reject the heritage that meant nothing to them but persecution and deprivation.

Some floaters might think that their ancestors who lived years ago were primitive, because they lacked formal education, and would be embarrassed to even think about them. Maybe their grandfather was a salesman who sold his wares door to door, or their grandmother stitched the holes in her neighbor's socks in order to buy a loaf of bread for her hungry children. Stories like that would leave the floater hopeless and fearful that maybe some of these primitive genes remained with him or his children. Every time he would see a photograph of a grim-looking man who obviously worked hard with his hands, digging into earth to plant the soil to grow potatoes for his children's supper, the floater would say, "I have no idea who this man is."

And the photographs together with the prayer books would collect dust, and wait.

But then one day the floater would wake up in the middle of the night when all were asleep, with the sudden knowledge that something was missing in his life. He would turn on the computer quietly and start searching, looking for his family history.

"Hello, anybody out there?" he would type into cyberspace. "Argentina, Australia, Austria, Hungary, Sweden, is anybody reading my message? I am looking for my family who lived in Pecs, near the border of Hungary and Romania, a little town with only a few Jewish families."

But there was no response. Nobody was there anymore to tell him stories. They were buried in Europe, or in America, or in the land of Israel, in Har Hamenuchot cemetery or on the Mount of Olives.

And then the floater would start typing names into the computer, trying to reconstruct the names that he had heard when he was a little child.

"Was it Grossman with one *s* or two? Did my father mention that he was raised on a chicken farm or was that my mother? No, my mother grew up in the city of Odessa where she was raised in a noble house. It must have been my father whose father was a farmer, or was he the one who locked himself into the local synagogue to study the Talmud?"

All these questions and nobody to answer them. During the time when mother and father, uncles and aunts were trying to reach him, he was not within reach. He was floating towards the new and the fresh which was offered to him while growing up in Boston or Berkeley, mesmerized by lecturers who preached from the pulpit to open minds and ears that were closed to all that was close.

At first the floater wanted to give up and announce to the world that he was alone with no foundation to stand on. He wanted to donate the photographs to the local Jewish museum so that others would stare at the faces he did not know anything about. Maybe they would feel the connection he could not. But the need had gripped him now and he started to ask people who were interested in family history.

And his past began to take shape, slowly. His great-grandfather became alive when the floater peeled off layer upon layer of history. This ancestor had eight children and ten grandchildren when the war broke out. Their names were Rafuel, Ethele, Feige, Rivkele, Menachem, Fraidl, Meushi, Chaya, Duvid and Efraim.

And the floater became grounded. He discovered his foundation, he rebuilt it, and in doing so he found true meaning in the collection of memories, stories and pictures. It's not too late, it's never too late.